CARS OF THE 1950s

pil

Publications International, Ltd.

Louis Weber, CEO
Publications International, Ltd.
8140 Lehigh Avenue
Morton Grove, IL 60053

Permission is never granted for commercial purposes.

ISBN: 978-1-63938-415-0

Manufactured in China.

8 7 6 5 4 3 2 1

Let's get social!
@Publications_International
@PublicationsInternational
www.pilbooks.com

CREDITS

The editors gratefully acknowledge the following people and organizations for images that helped make this book possible.

Acme Photo; Robert J. Anderson; Aston Martin Lagonda Limited; Roger D. Barnes; Scott Baxter; Ken Beebe; John Blake; BMW Group; Bugatti Automobiles S.A.S.; Buick Division of GM; Rob Burrington; Chan Bush; Cadillac Division of GM; California Department of Transportation; Craig Caugh; Chevrolet Division of GM; Chrysler Historical Collection; John Conde; Daimler AG; Mirco DeCet; Tony Eboli; Randy Edmonds; Ferrari S.p.A.; Al Ferreira; Steen Fleron; Ford Motor Company; Jim Frenak; Mitch Frumkin; Nina Fuller; Russ Garrett; General Motors Company; Paul W. Gillan; Thomas Glatch; GM Photographic; Jeff Godshall; Eddie Goldberger; David Gooley; Gary Greene; Sam Griffith; R. H. Gurr; Jerry Heasley; Don Heiny; Ronald C. Hill; S. Scott Hutchinson; Hutchinson Photo; Jaguar Land Rover Limited; David Jensen; Robin Jones; Bud Juneau; D. J. Kava; Laurel Kenney Jr.; Tim Kerwin; Milton Gene Kieft; Ron Kimball Photography; Koenigsegg Automotive AB; Lloyd Koening; Automobili Lamborghini S.p.A.; Rick Lenz; Ed Lobit; Randy Lorentzen; Dan Lyons; Vince Manocchi; McLaren Automotive; Ron McQueeney; Doug Mitchel; Ron Moorhead; Mike Mueller; The National Automotive Historical Collection, Detroit Public Library; David Newhardt; Nissan Motor Corporation; Neil Nissing; Eddie Noggles; Nina Padgett-Russin; Oldsmobile Division of GM; David Patryas; Frank Peiler; Pontiac Division of GM; Greg Price; Richard Quinn; Rob Reaser; Larry & Alice Richter; D. Randy Riggs; Jeff Rose; Dennis Rozanski; Bill Schintz Studio; Tom Shaw; Shelby American; Larry Shinoda; Shutterstock.com; Rick Simmons; Gary Smith; Mike Spenner; Richard Spiegelman; Steve Statham; Stellantis; Brooks Stevens; Tom Storm; David Suter; David Temple; Bob Tenney; Marvin Terrell; Gregory Thomas; Phil Toy; Toyota Motor Corporation; Ross Tse; United Press Photo; Dan Vecchio; Volkswagen AG; W. C. Waymack; Joseph Wherry; White Eagle Studio; Hub Willson; Nicky Wright; Vince Wright

CONTENTS

Introduction

Looking back, the Fifties are remembered as a decade of vitality, prosperity, and unabashed promise. Americans saw the economy zooming, babies booming—and the Cold War looming.

In our collective memories, at least, it was a time of innocence: of simple pleasures and basic values, linked with boundless enthusiasm. These were also years of profound change. Television overtook radio as the foremost influence on popular culture. Rock 'n' roll, unheard of as the decade opened, developed into a major force. Labor-saving devices filled the ranch-style homes of the growing suburbs. The Depression mentality finally was fading, elbowed aside by a "buy now, pay later" philosophy. Jobs were plentiful—until a recessionary downturn in 1958 took millions of upward-strivers by surprise.

For those smitten with the automotive fever, though, this was a singularly glorious epoch. Only Detroit had the cure, and its prescription was doled out every fall to great fanfare. TV sets broadcast the latest shapes, radios blared the car companies' catchy jingles. Young car buffs scanned magazine pages for pictures of the spanking-new mechanical attractions. Errands demanded an end run past dealers' row, just to see if the paper coverings had yet been torn down from the showroom windows to reveal the splendor of next year's models.

As the Fifties began, 40 million automobiles roamed American roads. In fact, three out of five families owned one. Automakers still were trying to satiate pent-up demand for new cars. Several independent makes had sprouted, notably Kaiser and Frazer. Others had been around since before World War II: Hudson, Nash, Packard, Studebaker, Willys. Imports trickled into American ports.

As manufacturers met—then exceeded—the nation's automotive appetite, sales began to sag. Ford and Chevrolet waged a price war in 1953 that injured the independents far more than the "Big Three" (General Motors, Ford Motor Company, and Chrysler Corporation). Kaiser sighed its last gasp in '55. Hudson and Packard soon followed. Nash diminished to its compact Rambler spinoff. Studebaker gained a temporary reprieve only by virtue of its well-timed '59 Lark compact.

Meanwhile, the horsepower race that had begun with the Rocket Oldsmobiles in '49, then escalated to Chrysler "Hemis" and Chevrolet V-8s, progressed into a leapfrogging bout. Cars, too, grew bigger—and presumably better, in a culture that tended to equate the two. Chrome oozed from every panel. Tailfins, having started small, sprouted beyond belief. The Edsel quickly came and went: a noble hope for 1958, a synonym for failure by '60.

Styling took over from engineering as the driving force behind sales. Automatic transmissions began to edge aside traditional stickshifts. Power gadgetry blos-somed, climaxing with Ford's elaborate retractable hardtops. Pillarless four-doors joined their two-door mates. Three-tone paint jobs appeared. Station wagons emerged as the vehicle of choice in growing suburbia.

This book presents it all. While automobiles serve as its hub, **Cars of the 1950s** provides a spirited romp through a period that's filled with fond memories for those who lived it, and inspires awe—and often disbelief—in the generations that came after. American cars exemplified the spirit of those times: brawny and proud, hopeful and boastful, strong and special. We hope you find this tribute to the '50s as colorful and stirring as the decade itself.

1950

America was changing rapidly as the 1950s began—and the pace was about to pick up. World War II had been over for half a decade. Memories of the Great Depression grew blurred. Families began their migration to the suburbs, which sprouted like tentacles around the nation's cities.

Veterans and civilians who'd endured privation in the past now faced a cornucopia of consumer goods—and were determined to enjoy the bounty. Women who'd toiled in factories and offices during the war resumed their roles as housewives, making Dad—more often than not—the sole breadwinner. Even with a single salary, though, most folks had money to spend. Incomes had risen steadily, despite a wave of strikes. Median family income topped $3300 a year.

Not every sign was positive. Unemployment hit 7 percent in January—up from 4.5 percent a year earlier, setting a postwar record. Still, the American Dream was simple enough: a good job, well-behaved family, pleasant home. Oh, and one more thing—an impressive automobile.

When World War II ended, automakers had nothing fresh to offer car-hungry Americans; they simply issued mildly revised prewar models. Studebaker was first with a completely new design, which debuted for 1947. By then, Henry Kaiser and Joe Frazer had joined forces, producing cars under both names. A year later, Hudson launched its low-slung "Step-down" design, and the new Cadillac body displayed the first tailfins. Chevrolet and Pontiac launched curvy new bodies for 1949. Ford chose a boxier (but tasteful) shape, while companions Lincoln and Mercury showed more roundness. Chrysler products stood steadfastly upright. Nash went wild, with an aerodynamic form that many said resembled an "upside-down bathtub." One new body style emerged, this from GM. Called the "hardtop convertible," it melded the vitality of a convertible with the practicality of a closed coupe.

Through the late '40s, demand was stronger than automakers could hope to fulfill. By 1950, though, nearly all designs were at least a year old, and the seller's market was subsiding. Manufacturers had to deliver something fresh, something exciting, if they hoped to continue the strong sales totals.

But not yet. With only a few exceptions, facelifts were the order of the year. Most 1950 models—Chevrolet and Plymouth to Hudson and Nash—showed little more than touch-ups. Studebaker's innovative "bullet nose," for instance, led a body that differed little from its predecessor.

Because truth in advertising was not yet an issue, automakers could claim their products were the handsomest, the most frugal—or simply the best, period. Pontiac, for instance, declared its dashboard "the most beautiful in the industry." Hudson called its cars "safest" (not without validity, in view of their rigid construction).

Without quite realizing it, Oldsmobile managed to set off a "horsepower race" that would overtake the industry. All the engineers did was create a shortstroke, overhead-valve V-8: the '49 Rocket engine. Far more efficient than inline and L-head engines that powered most cars, the ohv V-8 would become the engine of choice for a new breed of driver—the hot rodder—and for millions of ordinary Americans.

Quite a few automakers cut prices on 1950 models. As a result, a whopping 6,663,461 cars (8,004,242 total vehicles) were built—an all-time record, 30 percent above the '49 total. Meanwhile, the Federal Reserve Board placed stricter limits on credit—an issue destined to rise again as incomes trailed the public's urge for automobiles.

Americans finally were managing to forget war. Then, on June 25, President Truman ordered U.S. troops to Korea in a "police action" that would last for several years. Fear of wartime shortages triggered a car-buying frenzy. In December, a "state of emergency" was proclaimed.

Auto production never halted, as it had during World War II, but certain raw materials wound up in short supply, and makers faced output limits. No matter. As 150 million Americans thirsted for private transport, Detroit was eager to provide.

Chrysler Corporation

Chrysler got its start in 1924 when founder Walter P. Chrysler acquired the ailing Maxwell/Chalmers company, soon rechristening it with his own name. The company's mid-priced cars had hydraulic brakes well before most rivals, illustrating an emphasis on engineering that prevailed at Chrysler for decades to come. Dodge was acquired in 1928, followed by the introduction of the low-price Plymouth, mid-price DeSoto, and upper-crust Imperial. This lineup resulted in a price "ladder," mimicking that which had made General Motors—for whom Walter P. Chrysler had formerly worked—such a success.

Nash-like models from late 1948 were studies for possible early Fifties Chryslers.

Top Right: About as radical a Chrysler as could be found in the conservative 1950 lineup was the wood-trimmed Town & Country Newport hardtop coupe. Formerly a wood-structure convertible, the Town & Country now featured white-ash framing attached to steel body panels. Though prototype hardtops (without center roof pillars) were built a few years earlier, the 1950 models were the company's first production versions. This model's $4003 price topped even those of the luxury Imperials—by a lot. Only the low-production Crown Imperial limousines cost more. Upper-line Chryslers—Saratoga, New Yorker, Town & Country, and Imperial—rode a 131.5-inch wheelbase (Crown Imperial a 145.5-inch span)—and came with a 323-cubic-inch straight eight with 135 horsepower. Just 700 were built, this year only.

Bottom Right: By far the most popular 1950 Chrysler was this $2329 Windsor sedan. Comparable entry-level Royals cost a couple hundred dollars less. Windsor and Royal had a 125.5-inch wheelbase and a 250-cid six with 115 hp.

DeSoto's Custom Sportsman two-door hardtop shows off the reverse-slant roofline and three-piece rear window found on all Chrysler Corp. hardtops.

Lacking a true automatic transmission, Chrysler offered Fluid Drive starting in the early 1940s. Fluid Drive used a conventional manual transmission, but added a fluid coupling (a predecessor to today's torque converter) between the engine and clutch. The fluid coupling allowed the car to come to a stop and accelerate away in any gear without using the clutch, which was only needed to shift between gears. Fluid Drive was offered in several variations during the 1950s under a variety of names, including Fluid-Matic (Chrysler), Fluid Drive with Tip-Toe Shift (DeSoto), and Gyro-Matic (Dodge). The low-price Plymouth didn't get a version until 1953.

On the Chrysler Corporation ladder, DeSoto stood just below the top-rung Chrysler. The make had been named for Spanish explorer Hernando de Soto. Only two series were offered: DeLuxe and Custom. Most versions shared the Chrysler Windsor/Royal body, but had different styling and a smaller 236-cid six. This $2174 Custom sedan was the best seller. Interiors of a Custom DeSoto sedan were better appointed than those of the more utilitarian DeLuxe series. DeSoto promoted its cars' plentiful "hat room," as well as "big, wide doors [that] let you walk in... not wiggle in!"

Left: A couple of interesting bodies offered by DeSoto were the 139.5-inch-wheelbase, nine-passenger Suburban sedan with suicide (rear-hinged) back doors, and the wood-trimmed wagon. At $3179, the Suburban was the most costly DeSoto.

Dodge was second on the corporate ladder. The popular Meadowbrook sedan sat on a 123.5-inch wheelbase, listed for $1848, and, like all Dodges, came with a 230-cid six.

Plymouth was Chrysler Corporation's low-price brand that competed directly with Chevrolet and Ford, and was typically the nation's number-three seller behind those two. Plymouths were known as being solid and reliable, and the 118.5-inch wheel-base of all but the low-line Deluxe two-doors allowed for more interior room than Chevys and Fords with their shorter wheelbases. The $2372 Special Deluxe wood-bodied wagon was Plymouth's most expensive car and sold only 2057 copies. These "woodies" would soon be replaced by steel-bodied versions.

Above: Deluxe two-door models sat on a 111-inch wheelbase. Representing the cheapest Plymouth offered for 1950 was this $1371 Deluxe business coupe.

Left: Wayfarer was Dodge's 115-inch-wheelbase budget line. Top seller was the $1738 two-door sedan. The Wayfarer line also included a business coupe and the Sportabout convertible. Both only had a front bench seat.

Ford Motor Company

While Henry Ford didn't invent the automobile, his Model T of 1909-1927 was certainly instrumental in bringing it to the masses. Also monumental was the debut of Ford's famous flathead V-8 in 1932, an engine that would power the company's cars for two decades and become a favorite among hot-rodders.

In an effort to expand its market presence, Ford Motor Company purchased the luxury Lincoln brand in 1922, and brought out the mid-priced Mercury nameplate for 1939.

Henry Ford II (center), sometimes called "Henry the Deuce," took the reins of Ford Motor Company from his father in 1945. He hired a group of young engineers and executives known as the "Whiz Kids" to turn the ailing company around. Their efforts resulted in the redesigned 1949 models.

The '49 proved so successful that it wasn't altered much for 1950. Though Tudor (proper spelling) models were more popular, Fordor (also proper spelling) versions sold strongly, with prices starting at $1472. Buyers had a choice of a 226-cubic-inch 95-horsepower six or the venerable 239-cid 100-hp flathead V-8. Both were offered only with manual transmission. Ford competed against Chevrolet and Plymouth, a trio known as the "low-priced three."

Above: Deluxe and Custom trim levels were offered for 1950, but only the latter had a convertible, which was priced at $1886.

Right: The wood-bodied two-door Country Squire wagon was claimed to carry "8 big people in comfort" for $2119.

Ford didn't have a two-door hardtop to compete with Chevy's stylish new Bel Air, so at midyear it released a special Tudor, the two-tone vinyl-topped $1711 Crestliner. Ribbed fender skirts accented its sleek look. Priced $200 above a plain Custom Tudor, Crestliners came in three vivid two-tone blends, including Sportsman Green and black.

The desire to revive the Continental remained strong in the studio, as this coupe model attests.

Mercurys played in the mid-price field against the likes of DeSoto and Oldsmobile. Like their Ford siblings, Mercs were redesigned for 1949, and were equally successful. They were powered by a 239-cid version of the flathead V-8 rated at 110 hp. A Mercury similar to this $2412 convertible paced the 1950 Indy 500.

Lincoln competed in the luxury segment with Cadillac and Chrysler Imperial, falling between the two in sales. Prices started at $2529 for this base coupe. All Lincolns shared a 336-cid 154-hp flathead V-8. Newly optional was Hydra-Matic automatic transmission, which Lincoln purchased from General Motors.

Above: Lincoln's upper-crust Cosmopolitan rode a four-inch-longer wheelbase and featured distinctive front wheel well "eyebrows." This $3240 Sport Sedan shows off its "suicide" rear doors.

Left: Mercury coupes became a favorite of the hot-rod set, particularly after starring as James Dean's ride in the movie *Rebel Without a Cause*.

This Cortaro Red Metallic Monterey is topped by a black vinyl roof and features all-leather upholstery, options that together added $21 to the $2146 base price of 1950 Monterey.

General Motors

Monolithic General Motors was incorporated in 1908 by hard-charging William C. Durant, who brought together Buick (founded 1903), Oldsmobile (1897), and soon thereafter, Cadillac (1902) to form what would eventually become the world's largest corporation. Though Durant was ousted two years later, he went on to start Chevrolet in 1911, which grew quickly and was itself brought into the GM fold by 1918—along with Durant, who regained power. Pontiac was added along with four other "companion" makes during the 1920s, and was the only one of the quintet to survive past 1940. By that time, Durant was gone (again), and the helm was now in the hands of Alfred P. Sloan, who established the successful "price ladder" that drove GM to greatness and became the model for other car companies—most notably Chrysler Corp., and to a lesser extent, Ford Motor Company.

Buick's 1949 redesign included the first of the marque's signature "portholes" on the front fenders. The low-line Special and midline Super (shown in sedan form) got three on each side. A 1950 update brought a massive, bucktooth grille and a kick-up in the rear fender line. All models were powered by one of Buick's famous straight-eight engines. Spanning a price range of $1803 to $1983, the Special had a 248-cubic-inch version with 115/120 horsepower. Supers cost about $200 more and had a 263 with 124/128 hp.

Buick's top-line $2633 Roadmaster Riviera hardtop coupe got four portholes and a 322-cid eight with 152 hp. Roadmaster interiors ranked as "ultra regal." All models adopted a single-unit bumper/grille. Dynaflow, Buick's automatic transmission, was standard in Roadmasters and optional in other Buicks.

Middle: As in previous years, a fastback coupe was proposed for the entry-level Series 61. Developments on the ultimately discarded body style are shown in February.

Above: New for 1950 Cadillacs was a one-piece windshield, as shown on this $2761 hardtop coupe representing the Series 61 line—the least expensive Cadillacs offered. The flashier Series 62s cost about $200 more. Also offered was a lone Series Sixty Special sedan at $3828, and a line of low-production long-wheelbase Series 75 models priced at a whopping $4650 to $5170.

Chevy's new Bel Air was America's first low-price hardtop coupe at $1741. It was available in a variety of two-tone color schemes. The Bel Air was said to blend "the airiness [...] of a convertible with the coziness and permanence of an all-steel top."

Chevrolet represented the opposite end of the GM price spectrum, though this snazzy red Styleline Deluxe convertible hardly looks the part. At $1847 it was the most expensive 1950 Chevy, with lesser models starting as low as $1329.

This $1529 Styleline Deluxe sedan was Chevy's most popular car. It was available with the newly introduced two-speed Powerglide transmission, making it the only one of the "low-priced three" (Chevy, Ford, and Plymouth) to offer an automatic—a big advantage that was enough to vault Chevy into first place in the sales race: At nearly 1.5 million sold, it outgunned rival Ford by almost 300,000 units. Standard was a 92-hp 216-cid six, but Powerglide cars got a 105-hp 235.

To separate them from "lesser" Oldsmobiles, top-line 98s got peaked rear fenders hosting round taillights.

Perhaps more fitting of the "sporty" label was this racy 88 convertible.

Oldsmobile introduced America's first fully automatic transmission for 1940. Hydra-Matic was a stunning engineering coup, and was eventually used not only by other GM makes but by other car companies as well. With the introduction of its short-stroke, overhead-valve Rocket V-8 engine for 1949, Oldsmobile became not only a technology leader, but also a race-winner. The 303-cubic-inch 135-horsepower Rocket powered many an Olds 88 to victory on the stock-car tracks. It was also used in Oldsmobile's larger—and heavier—98. The bottom-line Olds 76 carried a 237-cid six making 105 hp. Oldsmobile prices ranged from $1719 to $2772. This sporty 88 Deluxe sedan went for $2056.

Pontiacs were powered by straight sixes and eights of 239/268 cid and 90 to 113 hp. They were priced from $1673 to the $2190 of this Chieftain Eight convertible, placing them between Chevrolet and Oldsmobile on the corporate ladder. Pontiacs were known for their chrome hood and trunklid strakes and gold chief's head hood ornaments.

Two-door hardtops appeared for 1950, introducing the Catalina name.

Hudson Motor Car Corporation

Hudson Motor Car Company was founded in 1909 by a group of businessmen that included Roy D. Chapin, Sr., and retailing magnate Joseph L. Hudson. The former became the company's first president; the latter lent his name to the product.

Though Hudson wasn't the first company to use what we now call unitized construction, it introduced a new twist with its redesigned 1948 models. Marketed as the "Step-down" design, it surrounded the passenger compartment with integrated frame girders, thus allowing the floor to be lower than in other cars of the day. This resulted in a high degree of passenger protection and a lower center of gravity. The latter was at least as responsible as the company's famed Twin H-Power six-cylinder engine in helping the Hudson Hornet rule the stock-car tracks in its heyday. Unfortunately, it also made the car expensive to update, a problem that would plague Hudson after the postwar seller's boom subsided in the early '50s.

Above: Hudson's 1948-vintage Step-down models were offered in Super and dressier Commodore trim with either a 262-cubic-inch flathead six or 254-cubic-inch flathead straight-eight engine. By 1950, the six produced 123 horsepower, the eight 128. Shown is the $2257 Commodore Six two-door coupe.

Top Right: For 1950, Hudson added the lower-price Pacemaker to its line. The cars rode a shorter wheelbase, carried a 232-cid six rated at 112 hp, and cost about $100 less than comparable "big" Hudsons. This $2428 Pacemaker Brougham convertible displays the heavy windshield header that distinguished Hudson convertibles. But because it was virtually impossible to restyle, Hudson had to stick with the same shape through '54. The new stripped-down, lower-priced Pacemaker line included a sedan, two coupes, two-door brougham, and convertible.

Millions asked for it...here it is!

THE LOWER-PRICED

New Hudson Pacemaker

WITH FAMOUS "STEP-DOWN" DESIGN

HUDSON MOTOR CAR COMPANY, DETROIT 14, MICHIGAN, U.S.A.

Even in a Pacemaker, passengers had plenty of head and elbow room. Hudson seats were a whopping 64 inches wide.

Kaiser-Frazer Corporation

Conceived during the postwar years when a shortage of new cars made it a seller's market, Kaiser-Frazer Corporation joined the fray as perhaps the most viable automaker among the growing number of independents. Founded by shipbuilder Henry J. Kaiser and super salesman Joseph W. Frazer, each lent their name to separate cars that were nearly identical save for trim variations and price. Kaisers and Frazers were rather large and expensive—roughly the size and cost of a top-line V-8 Oldsmobile 98—yet were powered by a lowly flat-head six-cylinder engine. If it weren't for the huge pent-up demand, it's doubtful the company would have even gotten off the ground. As it was, however, the pair sold a combined 140,000 cars in inaugural 1947, a strong showing.

Top: Noted industrial designer Brooks Stevens was hired to provide Frazer styling ideas. Drawings dated March 24, 1948 show his ideas for a prospective 1950 sedan with a low-mouth bumper/grille, and a convertible coupe.

Right: Another sedan proposal from October '48.

Top of Next Page: Stevens also drew up dramatic interior concepts.

Below: Kaiser beat most automakers to market with a four-door hardtop. Called the Virginian, it wasn't a true hardtop, as the center roof pillar was replaced by a framed glass pane that didn't roll down like the other windows. At $2995, it cost $800 more than a comparable sedan, and few were sold.

Above: Both Kaiser and Frazer sold leftover 1949 models as 1950s. Each line offered two trim levels, with Frazers being slightly pricier than comparable Kaisers. The '50 Frazer four-door sedan cost $2395 in standard form (shown), $200 more in uplevel Manhattan guise. All Kaiser-Frazer models were powered by a 226-cubic-inch flathead six designed by Continental but built by K-F; it produced 100 horsepower in low-line models, 112 in upper-line series.

Right: K-F was known for offering a wide variety of vivid exterior hues, and interiors of higher-line models in particular could be adorned with extensive chrome trim and rich, colorful fabrics.

Another innovative body style was the utility sedan, with an upper hatch lid and lower tailgate replacing the traditional trunklid. Folding the rear seat-back created a 10-foot long load area complete with wood floor ribbing. This Kaiser Vagabond retailed for $2288, just $93 more than a conventional sedan.

Nash Motors

After cutting his automotive teeth at General Motors, Charles W. Nash left the corporation in 1916 to form his own company and bring out a car under his own name. Nash built mainly mid-priced cars that often sported innovative features. Among them was the 1941 600, one of the earlier cars with unitized construction. These and other Nashes of the '40s carried somewhat unusual styling, but that changed in 1949 with the introduction of the "bathtub" Airflytes, which went from "unusual" to just plain weird.

Smooth where other cars of the day were lumpy, Airflytes looked—and were—aerodynamic. Aiding this in both appearance and fact were skirted fenders that made Nashes unmistakable, a signature trait they would maintain until the bitter end.

Top Left: It isn't hard to guess where the "bathtub" Airflytes got their nickname. Topping the 1950 Nash lineup were the long-wheelbase Ambassadors (shown), which came as two- and four-door sedans in a host of trim levels with prices ranging from $2039 to $2223. GM's Hydra-Matic automatic transmission was newly optional. Sharing the look, but on a shorter wheelbase, was the $1633 to $1897 Statesman.

Top Right: Nash claimed that the compact's version of unibodied Airflyte construction was "twice as rigid" as body-on-frame designs, "free of the usual squeaks and rattles." With a 100-inch wheelbase—15-inches shorter than Chevrolet's—Ramblers seemed to occupy a different world than their "bathtub" big brothers.

Middle: Ambassadors had a 234-cubic-inch six with 112 horsepower, Statesmans a 184-cid version with 82 hp. Both models were known for having seats that folded down into a bed.

Bottom Right: New for 1950 was the compact Rambler, which carried many "big Nash" styling cues. It was initially offered in two unusual body styles—a two-door all-steel wagon and a Landau convertible with fold-back top and stationary side windows—both priced at $1808 and powered by a 172-cid six with 82 hp.

Packard Motor Car Corporation

Sometimes it's hard to understand how a company that once so clearly dominated its market segment could sink so far so fast. Yet such was the case with Packard.

Started in 1899 by James Ward Packard, the company quickly grew to become a prominent automaker. By 1930 it was by far the most popular luxury make, with more than double the sales of Cadillac. And in 1940, it outsold "The Standard of the World" by a seven-to-one margin. It wasn't until after World War II that Cadillac finally caught it, and then the two companies played "who's in first" for a couple of years before Packard took a nosedive into oblivion.

Packard's top-line model for 1950 was the Custom Eight, offered only in four-door sedan and convertible forms. Production was very limited: just 707 of the $3875 sedans, and only 77 of the $4570 convertibles.

Introduced in late 1949 was Ultramatic Drive, Packard's first automatic transmission.

The standard Eight delivered a silken ride in a plush interior.

Packard's volume car was called simply the "Eight." Riding a shorter wheelbase than other models, it was offered in two- and four-door sedans priced from $2224 to $2383, along with a $3449 "woody" wagon.

A 1950 Packard brochure shows the complete lineup. Entry-level Eights wore a horizontal-bar grille, top-line Customs a crosshatch grille. In between sat the midline Supers, which rode the longer wheelbase and had mixed grille patterns: Base Supers had the Eight's grille, Deluxe models the Custom's grille. Due to their bulbous styling, Packards of this era were often derided as "pregnant elephants." Note Packard's famous cormorant hood ornament, which is depicted only slightly out of scale in these illustrations. All Packards were powered by a flathead straight-eight engine, but in different displacements and power ratings for each series. The Eight's 288-cubic-inch version made 135 horsepower, the Super's 327 had 150 hp, and the Custom's 356 made 160 hp—the most offered in an American car for 1950.

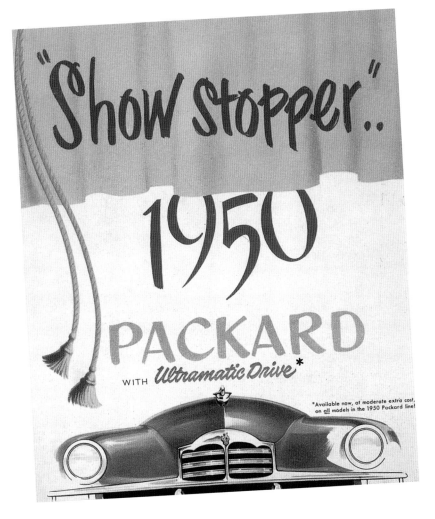

Studebaker Corporation

Established in 1852 as a wagon maker, Studebaker began building cars in 1902. Early models spanned a broad price range, but by the 1940s, six-cylinder Studebakers were selling for Chevrolet prices, while eights were closer to Buick territory.

For the most part, Studebakers of the era displayed rather conventional styling—until 1950, when the famed "bullet-nose" appeared. Though controversial, the new look proved wildly popular, catapulting Studebaker from eleventh to eighth in industry sales virtually overnight. By this time, eight-cylinder versions had departed, leaving just a pair of economical sixes—though not for long.

Top Left: This late-Forties small-scale model was an early indicator of the "bullet-nose" look that would distinctively identify Studebakers in 1950 and '51. Its finned fanjet beak might have been more industrial looking than the more-streamlined "propeller spinner" detail ultimately selected for production, but it could have served as an avant-garde symbol of the jet age that was coming to aviation.

Top Right: The model also featured a fastback roof then so much in vogue, but with a twist: a hatchback deck.

Styled to resemble the nose of an airplane, Studebaker's radical 1950 front end may look odd in today's light, but was a raging success at its introduction—and helped the company reach a record 320,000 sales. Also helping was Studebaker's first automatic transmission, optional on all models. The entry-level, 113-inch-wheelbase Champion line was powered by a 169-cubic-inch six rated at 85 horsepower; it's represented here by a $1981 Regal Deluxe convertible.

Midpriced Commanders had a 120-inch wheelbase and a 245-cid six with 102 hp. That same engine powered the range-topping 124-inch-wheelbase Land Cruiser, shown here in $2187 four-door sedan form.

The Champion's fuel economy is stressed in this ad. Its engine was much smaller than those in Chevrolets and Plymouths, and the Champion weighed less, too.

The 1950 Commander convertible with Bob Bourke's "bullet-nose" facelift of the 1947-49 bodies.

Studebaker prices started at $1419 for this Champion Custom three-passenger coupe, putting it on par with the cheapest Chevys, Fords, and Plymouths.

The New Jersey and Pennsylvania Turn-pikes opened for business in '51, and the traditional nickel phone call now cost a dime in some cities. Parents began to feel guilty if their offspring didn't have music lessons and a set of encyclopedias, as the nation turned its focus toward kids—as well as teenagers.

Prosperity and optimism persisted. Unemployment dipped to 3.3 percent, while the gross national product grew by 15 percent. More than three-fourths of cars sold were considered "deluxe" mod-els, as average family income continued its upward climb—now topping $3700 a year. Americans began to indulge in an infatuation with chrome—an idiosyncrasy destined to last several decades. Growing use of two-toning also added sales appeal.

I Love Lucy appeared on TV screens for the first time, as did *The Cisco Kid* and Dinah Shore's *Chevy Show*. Color broadcasts were successful, but programs would be black-and-white a while longer.

At first glance, "More of the same" might have been the automotive slogan for

1951. With the exception of totally re-designed Kaisers and Packards, nearly all automobiles saw little more than touch-up work: a fresh grille here, revised taillights there, brightwork moved or modified.

In the wake of Nash's success with the Rambler, Kaiser launched a new compact: the Henry J, powered by Willys engines. Henry J. Kaiser insisted that the public didn't want a truly small car, but rather one "of conventional size with enough modern styling distinction to instill pride of ownership."

Chrysler joined the horsepower race by issuing a 180-horsepower Hemi V-8. Hud-son unleashed the Hornet—a car destined to trounce the competition on the stock-car circuit—with the biggest six-cylinder engine on the market adding vigor to the roadholding skills of the "Step-down" design.

Hardtop coupes joined Ford and Plymouth lineups, as well as Hudson's and Packard's. As the hardtops gained popularity, true convertibles declined.

Not every car came with turn signals or backup lights in the early Fifties. Drivers still proclaimed their intentions to others via hand signals.

As the Korean War intensified, production cutbacks were ordered by the National Production Authority—despite insistence by the National Automobile Dealers Association that cars were necessities. Chrome trim became thinner, curtailment of nickel limited stainless-steel brightwork, and output of steel itself was slashed by 35 percent at midyear. Whitewall-tire production was halted in order to conserve natural rubber supply.

After more than half a century of production, the 100-millionth American car was built in December. Concern about the future, on the other hand, induced some Americans to hoard consumer goods—just in case of rationing or shortages.

A Roper survey found that an "alarming" number of Americans did not trust car dealers—though most were less critical of their own dealers. Bootlegging was widespread—not of liquor (as in the 1919-33 Prohibition era), but of new cars. In this "gray market," a legacy of the postwar boom, used-car dealers and fly-by-night vendors managed to obtain cars and steal sales from established dealerships, typically undercutting prices.

Because many folks were unable to participate in the hot new-car market, used-car dealers also enjoyed a busy year. Still, the average used car sold for $830—hardly a giveaway sum—and prices were "frozen" during the year to prevent further hikes.

As Detroit marked its 250th anniversary, small cars were arriving from Europe. Not just exciting sports cars, but tiny sedans: Anglias, Austins, Hillmans—plus a growing number of Volkswagens, foretelling a near future import revolution.

Chrysler Corporation

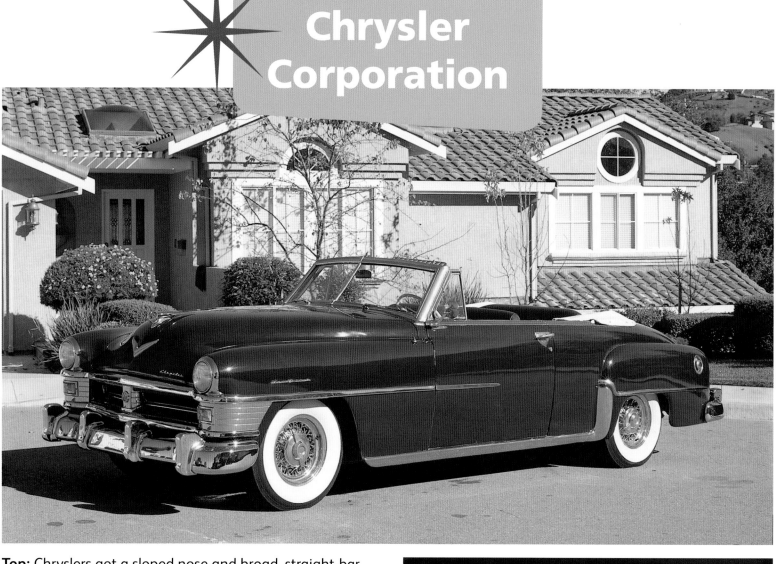

Top: Chryslers got a sloped nose and broad, straight-bar grille for 1951, but appearance changes took a back seat to the year's mechanical refinements. This big, flashy New Yorker convertible set its buyer back nearly $4000.

Right: By far Chrysler's biggest news of the year was the introduction of the powerful hemi-head V-8, which would soon become a legend. Nicknamed for its hemispherically shaped combustion chambers, the "Hemi" featured large valves flanking a centrally mounted spark plug that helped produce complete, even-burning combustion. In its debut season, the Hemi displaced 331 cubic inches and produced a whopping 180 horsepower. Cadillac's V-8 of the same displacement only produced 160. The Hemi powered all models save the base Windsor, which carried over its 250-cid six. The quickest Chrysler was the lightweight Saratoga, which won the stock class in the 1951 Mexican Road Race.

Top: Chrysler offered its first steel-bodied station wagons for 1950; they were sold alongside wood-bodied wagons, which were introduced in mid 1949. By '51, the woodies were gone. The remaining steel-bodied versions were given the Town & Country designation—a name that previously graced a wood-paneled two-door hardtop.

Above: Topping Chrysler's standard line was the luxurious Imperial, with "interiors of breathtaking elegance." Shown is the most expensive model, the $4402 convertible. Its padded leather-covered dashtop—termed the Safety Crash Pad—was an industry first.

Crown Imperials rode a longer wheelbase and came only as eight-passenger sedans priced in the $6600 range. Fewer than 500 were sold.

DeSoto got Chrysler's sloping nose for 1951, but not its Hemi engine—at least, not yet. For now, buyers had to make do with an enlarged 250-cubic-inch six. DeSoto's toothy grille became a favorite of the custom-car crowd.

Neither the slab-sided styling alternatives nor the one-piece windshield of this October 1948 clay model found their way onto early Fifties Dodges.

Dodges also got a sloped hood for 1951, along with a simpler grille. The bottom-line Wayfarer convertible and two-door sedan each cost around $1930.

By contrast, Plymouth's cheapest convertible was the $2222 Cranbrook. Plymouth was a less prestigious make than Dodge, but this car offered a rear seat that the Wayfarer ragtop didn't—along with a few extra amenities.

Plymouths were low-cost cars, yet it was the line-topping $1826 Cranbrook sedan that sold the best. A midline Cambridge sedan cost about $100 less; the low-line Concord series didn't offer a sedan.

Ford Motor Company

For 1951, Ford finally got a hardtop to compete with Chevy's Bel Air—and the new Plymouth Belvedere. Called the Victoria, it came only with a V-8 for $1925—$24 less than the convertible on which it was based. Gerdon Buehrig earned credit for the body.

Ford also caught up with Chevy in the transmission race with fully automatic Ford-O-Matic. Chevy had introduced the Powerglide for 1950; Plymouth wouldn't get an automatic until '54. The '51 Fords got a revised grille that replaced the former central "spinner" with two smaller ones, as shown on this $1553 Custom Fordor sedan.

Looking right at home in this beach scene is a $2029 Country Squire "woody" wagon. A total of 29,017 were built.

The most expensive ship in Lincoln's 1951 fleet was the $3891 Cosmopolitan convertible. Note the revised side trim, which was now shared with lesser Lincolns.

The most popular Lincoln was the base $2553 Sport Sedan.

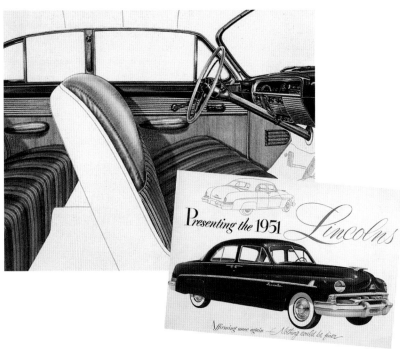

A dressy Capri edition of the Cosmopolitan two-door coupe brought "the ultimate in fine-car styling and coach work"—all for just $3350. Capri interiors featured custom-tailored cord and leather upholstery. Formerly woodgrained, Lincoln dashboards now were painted to match the body color.

Top: Capris came in a choice of three colors, with harmonizing "vinyl-leather" roofs. Cosmopolitans added a full-length sidespear, replacing the controversial airfoil trim.

Middle: A similarly dressed version of the base Lincoln coupe was the $2702 Lido.

Bottom: Nineteen fifty-one would prove to be the final year for Mercury's two-door woody wagon. At $2530, it carried the loftiest list price of any '51 Merc.

Mercury got its own version of Ford's fully automatic Ford-O-Matic transmission for 1951 called—you guessed it—Merc-O-Matic. It was a big deal to Mercury dealers, who had been losing business to "automatic" rivals.

Buyers could purchase a Mercury coupe for as little as $1947. By contrast, the local Ford dealer could sell a Tudor for about $500 less.

General Motors

Buick's former bucktooth grille was tamed a bit for 1951. The three front-fender portholes (officially called VentiPorts) identify this convertible as either a Special or Super, as the top-line Roadmaster had four. For those gripped by suspense, it's the $2728 Super. Note the "Dynaflow" badge on the rear fender. Dynaflow was Buick's automatic transmission. Its torque converter made it very smooth in operation, but because of its intended slippage (and resulting hindrance to performance) some detractors derided it as the "Dynaslush."

Cadillacs changed little in appearance for 1951, though all now came standard with Hydra-Matic, GM's (originally Oldsmobile's) four-speed automatic transmission. The stately Series 62 is represented by a $3987 convertible.

Above: Except for interior trim, the basic Series 62 hardtop was similar to a $3843 Coupe de Ville hardtop.

Right: Chevys got a mild "taillift" for 1951, with rear fenders that were squared off at the trailing edge. By this time, all GM makes except Chevrolet had dropped their four-door fastbacks due to slowing sales, and Chevy's would join them after this year. A two-door version would hold out a year longer. Fastbacks were called Fleetlines, and are represented here by a very rare $1594 Fleetline Special four-door.

Below: Styleline Special was the Fleetline's notchback counterpart, which sold for the same price but was far more popular. This Styleline Special two-door sedan went for $1540.

Bottom: Oldsmobile dropped its six-cylinder engine for '51, so all models carried a Rocket V-8. Added that year was the midline Super 88, shown here in $2328 four-door sedan guise.

The big Olds 98 again featured a unique taillight and side-trim treatment. Shown is the Holiday hardtop coupe.

Above: A drawing from April '46 for a new steel-bodied station wagon. Pontiac built wagons to this basic design from 1949 to 1952, but only with four doors.

Left: Pontiac celebrated its 25th anniversary in 1951 with a very mild facelift.

Hudson Motor Car Corporation

Hudson greeted 1951 with a new arched grille, and offered General Motors' Hydra-Matic automatic transmission as an option. But the big news was the introduction of what would become a stock-car legend: the Hornet. Based on the longer Super/Commodore chassis, the Hornet's distinguishing feature was a huge 308-cubic-inch version of the flathead six, making it the biggest six of the era. It put out 145 horsepower, 17 more than the company's smaller straight-eight, and ten more than Oldsmobile's renowned overhead-valve V-8. This newfound power, combined with the Step-down's lower center of gravity and superior handling, resulted in the first of what would become a long string of stock-car racing victories. This Hornet four-door sedan listed for $2568.

Hornets begin to earn a long list of stock-car race victories and would prove to be nearly invincible from 1951-54.

Also new for '51 was a two-door hardtop body style, which gave the big Hudsons a much airier look. It was offered in all series except the low-price Pacemaker; shown is the $2869 Hornet version.

Kaiser-Frazer Corporation

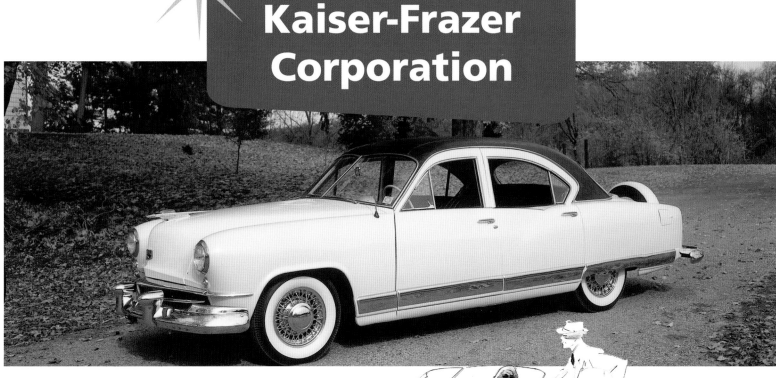

Top: A 1951 restyle with dipped beltline, squared-off rear fenders, and oddly shaped rear roof pillars gave Kaisers a fresh look. Also new that year was a Dragon trim option—shown here—that included special exterior colors, a padded vinyl top, and alligator-look vinyl interior.

Middle: The head of the Kaiser styling studio, Buzz Grisinger, drew this proposal for a convertible off Dutch Darrin's '51 Kaiser design.

Bottom: Sleek and sure-footed, the '51s still ran with the adapted industrial engine once used to power forklifts. This Traveler Deluxe two-door shows its graceful grille and dipped "sweetheart" windshield.

Top: Salesmen made effective use of the Traveler, seen here in four-door form.

Bottom: The '51 Kaiser had the lowest beltline and greatest glass area, industrywide. This Special two-door sedan has the signature dipped backlight.

Top: Frazers were also restyled for 1951, but this time, there was more distinction between the two makes. Frazer belatedly got a four-door hardtop, the $3075 Manhattan. It joined a convertible version—by then the only four-door ragtop on the market besides the similar Kaiser version—that had sold in very small numbers since 1949. Also newly available was GM's Hydra-Matic automatic transmission. However, none of this was enough to keep Frazer alive, and the name faded away after '51.

Upper Right: Vagabond utility sedans appeared for '51, even though Joe Frazer had not wanted them for his uplevel nameplate. Note the fendertop taillights.

Lower Right: Henry J. Kaiser felt a compact would give him a car the Big Three didn't offer, and since he'd already used the name "Kaiser," he called this one… the "Henry J." It arrived for 1951 in four- and six-cylinder versions priced from $1363 to $1499. First-year sales topped 80,000 units, but it would be all downhill from there.

Bottom: Consultant Dutch Darrin pushed this small-car design derived from his work on the '51 Kaiser.

Nash Motors

Though they aided aerodynamics and contributed to the car's unique look, the Rambler's skirted fenders made for a large turning circle and cumbersome flat-tire changes—problems that also afflicted the larger Nashes, and for the same reason. At $1993, the 1951 Rambler convertible sold surprisingly well considering a full-size Chevrolet convertible cost only $37 more.

There was a greater price spread between a 1951 Rambler wagon and those sold by the Big Three—mostly because the Big Three's were all "woodys." This Rambler Custom went for $1993, but the cheaper Super was just $1885. By contrast, Big Three wagons ranged from $2029 to $2191.

New to the Rambler lineup for '51 was the $1968 Custom Country Club hardtop coupe. It introduced the reverse-slant rear roof pillar that would later appear in Nash's larger cars.

Nash Presents the World's Most Modern Cars, the 1951 Airflytes

A definite family resemblance can be seen in this 1951 Nash brochure showing (left to right) a Rambler, Statesman, and Ambassador.

A 1951 facelift brought big Nashes a vertical-bar grille (in place of crosshatch) and peaked rear fenders.

A collaborative effort between Nash and Donald Healey of England resulted in the aptly named Nash-Healey sports car. With an aluminum body and 125-horsepower version of the Ambassador engine, it was a vivid performer, but just 104 were sold at a steep $4063.

Packard Motor Car Corporation

Packards boasted an all-new look for 1951 that earned them "the most beautiful car of the year" award from the Society of Motion Picture Art Directors. The redesign more than doubled sales, but the company still slightly trailed Cadillac. Packards also got new model names. The base series was now the 200, followed by the 250, 300, and top-line Patrician 400. The 200 and 250 sat on a shorter wheelbase than the 300 and 400. Engines carried over, though the big 356-cubic-inch eight was dropped. The 200 had the 288 cid with 135 hp, all others the 327 with 150-155 hp.

Above: A new body style was the Mayfair hardtop coupe, available only in the 250 series for $3234. Note the wrap-around three-piece rear window, a feature on many makes.

Bottom: The top-line Patrician 400 could be identified by its added chrome trim and different taillight treatment. It came only as this $3662 four-door sedan, with a 155-horsepower, 327-cid straight-eight and Ultramatic.

Studebaker Corporation

The '51 Studebaker Commander's restyled grille looked as though it was smiling, and for good reason: Behind it lay a new overhead-valve V-8. Sized at 232 cubic inches, it put out 120 horsepower, making the Commander a weakling no more. The long-wheelbase Land Cruiser sedan enjoyed the same changes. Champions got the grille but not the V-8, as they retained their old 169-cid flathead six. Note this car's "suicide" rear doors, which had been adopted by all Studebaker four-door sedans in the 1950 redesign.

Above: A '51 Champion two-door sedan with bigger, brighter grillework and an add-on bumper bar. Part of the "bullet" surround was now body color.

Below: An interesting body style offered by Studebaker was the Starlight coupe, with its wraparound, four-piece rear window. Some questioned whether the cars were "coming or going," but there was little question that they were unique. The coupe was offered in the Champion (shown) and Commander lines in a total of five trim levels, with prices ranging from $1561 to $2137.

1952

Despite the Korean War, Americans considered themselves to be prospering. They were, too, as judged by continually rising incomes and modest unemployment—down as low as three percent.

Median family income approached $3900 a year, and the average full-time worker earned just over $3400—just about the price of a Packard convertible (or a pair of Fords).

Three out of five families had a car, and two-thirds of homes had telephones. Already, one in three American households watched television—perhaps with one of the new TV trays propped in front of each family member. The traditional evening ritual of eating—and conversing—around the dinner table was in jeopardy.

The family automobile was turning into an extension of the home. More and more cars were loaded with comforts and conveniences, from power steering and sofa-plush seats to outside mirrors and even the new automatic-dimming headlights. Radios, on the other hand, were AM-only, just as they were in most homes, and no-

body thought—yet—about playing music recordings in an automobile.

Some 56 million viewers saw vice-presidential candidate Richard Nixon's "Checkers" speech. Dwight Eisenhower trounced Adlai Stevenson in the presidential election.

Fast-food restaurants had been scattered around the country for years, but Americans were taking a fresh interest in no-wait service. Some of the new drive-ins even had carhops to take orders right at car-side, and deliver the food on trays that hooked onto the open car window.

Anxious Americans began to scan the skies for (alleged) flying saucers, entertain themselves with new Paint-by-Numbers kits, or peruse *Mad* magazine. Travelers might stay at one of the new Holiday Inns. On a less pleasant note, the scourge of polio hit more than 50,000, subversives were barred from teaching in public schools, and unions—including auto workers— were accused of harboring "Reds."

The Korean conflict placed a limit on auto production. As a rule, most automakers were restricted to 80 percent of their output in 1950. The National Production Authority set a specific limit of 4,342,000 cars, and actual calendar-year output turned out to be just a few thousand cars under that figure. Price ceilings were in effect, too.

Cadillac upped the output of its V-8 to 190 horsepower, complete with dual exhausts. Ford launched an overhead-valve six, Lincoln got a new ohv V-8, and Hudson adopted Twin H-Power (a fancy designation for twin carburetors).

Ford came out with a totally redesigned line of cars, while each rival made do with facelifts. Shoppers could even buy a car at Sears: the new Allstate, a thinly-disguised clone of the Henry J.

More than two million automatic transmissions were installed, despite a temporary limit, early in the model year, on the number of cars that could have automatic. One-third of cars had a V-8 engine. Sixes would hang on for many more years, but straight-eights were nearing the end of their era. Automotive gadgets proliferated, as aftermarket manufacturers had their inventors ponder more and more comforts and conveniences.

At a typical gas station, regular fuel cost about a quarter a gallon—considerably more than today, when allowance is made for inflation. In May, government limits on credit were dropped, with 24-month finance terms seen likely. Dealers anticipated a serious upswing in sales if customers could spread their payments over a longer period.

No new models debuted until November '51, and many waited until early 1952. Some experts recommended a return to autumn launches, which had been the rule before World War II.

Prosperous or not, Americans weren't able—or willing—to snap up everything the automakers produced. In contrast to the recent past, when they were able to sell every last vehicle the factories turned out—with a hefty profit—dealers were seeing cars languish on the lots. Kaiser, in fact, touched up thousands of leftover '51s and remarketed them as '52 models, until a mildly redesigned replacement was ready.

In some dealers' minds—and in the plans of certain Detroit executives—the answer to a buyer's market was obvious: Sell 'em hard, and move the merchandise at any cost. The industry was preparing for a sales blitz, a full-scale assault on the consumer led by Ford and Chevrolet, whose repercussions are still felt today.

Chrysler Corporation

Top: The 1952 Imperial served notice that the "three-box" look was fading.

Above: The "Beautiful Chrysler" may have been the New Yorker, but the fast Chrysler was the Saratoga. It combined the Windsor's shorter, lighter body with the New Yorker's 331-cubic-inch 180-horsepower Hemi V-8.

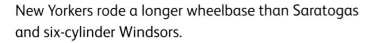

New Yorkers rode a longer wheelbase than Saratogas and six-cylinder Windsors.

DeSoto got its own version of the Hemi engine. Named FireDome, this scaled-down 276.1-cid V-8 yielded 160 horsepower—20 fewer than Chrysler's, but equal to the output of the new Lincoln. This $3183 FireDome Eight convertible promised 160-bhp performance, full power steering, and power braking.

The Hemi found its way into DeSotos for 1952, but in a smaller form: 276 cid and 160 hp. Otherwise, the '52 DeSoto was so much like the '51 version that Chrysler Corp. didn't even keep separate sales figures.

In the conformity of quickly expanding suburbia, neighbors' opinions mattered. Ad writers assured potential buyers that a $2908 Coronet Sierra station wagon would meet with everyone's approval.

Indeed, most folks would have to stare at a '52 Dodge—if they wanted to see any differences from '51. Only detail changes marked the new model year.

Plymouth likewise didn't change much for 1952—unless you consider including the make's name above the trunklid handle a major alteration.

Material shortages prompted by the Korean War resulted in lower production—and higher prices. This virtually un-changed Cranbrook convertible went up by more than $100 to $2329. Prices would be rolled back for '53.

Ford Motor Company

Top: This small-scale clay model from 1949 shows a few touches that would be picked up for the 1952 Fords, such as a one-piece windshield and a flared stamping in the rear body-sides. The "spinner" grille, a prominent feature of the '49 Ford, was expected to be carried on.

Above: Ford Motor Company was the only corporation to restyle all of its cars for 1952. But Ford ads pointed out that a fresh look wasn't the only thing that was new. A reengineered 215-cubic-inch overhead-valve Mileage Maker six was smaller in displacement than the previous six, but at 101 horsepower, had more guts. Meanwhile, the 239-cid flathead V-8 added ten ponies for a total of 110.

A string of brand spankin' new 1952 Fords are shown rolling off the Dearborn assembly line.

Some felt Ford's 1949 restyle hadn't yet worn out its welcome, but the '52 models truly looked advanced. Returning from 1950 was the central-mounted grille spinner, but the rest of the car was unmistakably new, with a squared-up profile and protruding head- and taillights. A Crestline Victoria hardtop coupe cost $1925. Skirts and a dealer-installed chrome strip above the side sculpture are add-ons.

For another $102, a Crestline buyer could go topless.

Ford's first all-steel wagons appeared for 1952, but they weren't cheap: a Country Squire was $2186.

This 1952 Sunliner's new round taillamps were destined to become a Ford styling trademark.

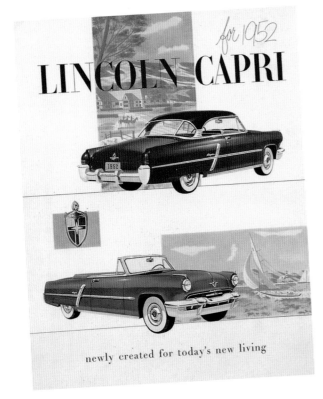

Sales didn't reflect it, but Lincoln was all new for '52. Aside from its vertical taillights, it reflected the same styling themes as its humble Ford stablemate—which may have been part of the problem. But it also got a new 317-cubic-inch overhead-valve V-8 with 160 horsepower, and that was definitely not part of the problem: This engine powered a quartet of Lincolns to a 1-2-3-4 finish in the grueling Carrera Panamericana road race, a truly amazing feat. Capri was now the top-line model, the convertible version of which sold for $3665.

Only 1191 Lincoln Capri convertibles were built, versus 5681 hardtops. William Schmidt led the styling team, while Earle S. MacPherson (later to develop MacPherson struts) helped with engineering. Lincoln's integrated bumper/grille became a styling trend, as did the gas filler hidden behind the license plate. In the sales race, Lincoln aimed less at Cadillac than at buyers of big Ninety-Eight Oldsmobiles.

Cosmopolitan became the entry-level Lincoln, this four-door sedan being the cheapest at $3198. Added to both lines was a new two-door hardtop.

Like Ford, Mercury shifted to all-steel wagons for 1952. For those who had difficulty accepting the transition, both companies offered woodgrain appliqués and trim to soothe their nerves. There were no more two-door wagons, but the four-doors came with a choice of six- or eight-passenger seating. They started at $2525 and $2570, respectively. For '52, the flathead V-8 was coaxed to 125 horses.

A 1952 ad points out that Mercury won its class in the Mobilgas Economy Run—three years in a row. It also claims the cars "won't be dated for years"—probably a safe bet, since they'd just been redesigned.

"We built a new car and made this challenge: Match Mercury if you can," said another ad. Those tough words were met with a huge drop in sales and a fall from sixth place to eighth in the industry. Oops.

General Motors

Buicks gained tiny chrome tailfins and revised side trim for 1952, but were otherwise little-changed. A Super convertible was $2869.

Buick's "woody" wagons saw very limited production during these years, mostly due to their high price. This Super wagon cost $3296 and sold just 1641 copies. In Roadmaster form, it went for the princely sum of $3977—making it far and away Buick's most expensive car—and attracted only 359 well-heeled buyers.

Cadillac celebrated its golden anniversary in 1952 still entrenched as the country's best-selling luxury make, despite negligible styling changes. Sales may have gotten a little boost, however, thanks to a power increase that bumped the 331-cubic-inch V-8 from 160 horses to 190—making it the most potent engine in the industry. Another "boost" came in the form of newly available power steering, a feature shared with Oldsmobile. Also new was Autronic Eye, which automatically dimmed the high beams when it detected the headlights of oncoming traffic. The "low-line" Series 61 was dropped for 1952, leaving the Series 62 as the entry-level model. A Series 62 Coupe de Ville hardtop could be parked in your driveway for $4013.

Top: This convertible's gold hood "V" signified Caddy's 50th anniversary.

Above: A Series 62 convertible cost $150 more—a small price to pay for what many believed was the ultimate in open-air motoring.

Side trim on Series 62s, like the two-door hardtop, was unchanged from 1951.

This concurrent upper-level convertible mock-up displays grille teeth similar to those adopted for 1952 production. The single-pane windshield would have to wait, though.

Top: Chevrolets were little-changed for 1952, yet easily remained number one in U.S. sales. One of the more popular models was this $1761 Styleline Deluxe sedan.

Middle: A $2673 Super 88 Holiday hardtop coupe could be optioned with newly available power steering and Autronic Eye automatic headlight dimmer, both shared with Cadillac.

Right: Considering Chevy's low-price status, the sporty but comparatively expensive Bel Air two-door hardtop sold an impressive 74,000 copies at $2006. Stick shift models kept the 92-horsepower engine, while Powerglide again brought the bigger truck-based six, with 105 horses and a new automatic choke.

Left: Super 88s (shown in four-door-sedan form) and 98s (now spelled out as "Ninety-Eight") enjoyed a 25-horse-power boost for '52, bringing the total to 160.

Below: Pontiacs again saw few changes for the new year, yet retained their stranglehold on the number-five sales position. A 122-hp Chieftain Eight Super Deluxe Catalina hardtop coupe cost a lot of breath to say, but only $2446 to buy.

A dummy scoop atop the grille and new wheel covers came for '52.

Hudson Motor Car Corporation

Above: Though the two-door hardtop was flashier, the lighter, cheaper two-door club coupe was the hot Hornet to have—and what most racers drove on the track. However, "cheaper" was relative; this '52 Hornet club coupe listed for $2742 ($353 less than the hardtop), which made it about $400 more than an Oldsmobile Super 88, and nearly $300 more than a Buick Super hardtop. Replacing Hudson's own "Super"—the Super Six—was the Wasp. Built on the shorter Pacemaker wheelbase but powered by the larger 262-cid six from the Commodore Six, it offered performance second only to the Hornet in Hudson's line at nearly $300 less. In a 1952 styling change, taillights went from vertical to horizontal.

Middle Right: Hudson took "only" 13 stock-car victories during 1951, but racked up a stunning 49 wins in 1952. No doubt the introduction of the company's Twin H-Power dual carburetor setup had something to do with that. Most often fitted to the Hornet's 308-cubic-inch six, it gave Hudson yet another advantage on the track.

Bottom Right: Hudson promised "jet-like acceleration" from Twin H-Power engine. Every engine sported bright red air cleaners.

Kaiser-Frazer Corporation

Kaisers displayed a revised grille and model line for '52, but little else was new. This top-line Manhattan (a name borrowed from defunct Frazer) went for $2654. Chrome plating during the Korean War was thinner than usual.

Above Left: This Herb Weissinger idea for a grille found its way onto Henry Js sold from mid 1952 through 1954.

Above Right: Proposed taillight style for the 1952 facelift.

Nash Motors

Above Left: An early rendering includes versions of final production details for '52, such as a grille of thick vertical teeth and a grooved beltline indentation atop the doors.

Above Right: Models and a full-size drawing show proposed design details. The boatlike profile was rejected for a smoother look.

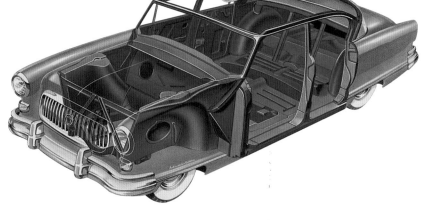

In celebration of Nash's 50th anniversary, the redesigned 1952 full-size models were promoted as "Golden Airflytes," though they appeared to take a step backward in the aerodynamics department. Styled in part by the famed Italian design house of Pinin Farina, they kept Nash's trademark unibody construction and skirted fenders, but adopted a squarer profile and a conventional roofline with reverse-slant rear window. Added to the line was a two-door hard-top. Ambassadors got a power boost via a larger 252-cubic-inch six with 120 horsepower.

Nash managers preferred the car their stylists had designed for 1952, but found it wise from a publicity standpoint to incorporate some of Pinin Farina's ideas and attribute the car's design to the Italian. A reverse-angle rear-roof pillar was one of the changes made. The Statesman was the smaller of the two senior Nash lines.

Above and Bottom Left: This Statesman Custom four-door sedan cost $2332 with its 88-hp six.

Nash dubbed its open Rambler a "convertible sedan," promising not only safety and rattle-proof construction but "dazzling performance, featherlight handling, down-to-earth economy." Its price rose to $2119.

Unlike their big brothers, the little Ramblers didn't change much for 1952.

Though the small sales volume could hardly justify it, the Nash-Healey was restyled for '52. Another Pinin Farina effort, it had a steel body with a one-piece windshield, headlights moved inboard and encircled by an oval grille, and a kick-up added to the rear fenders. A Nash-Healey won its class at LeMans.

Packard Motor Car Corporation

Packard FOR '52

Top Left: Aside from newly available power steering, Packards carried into 1952 with few changes. Now that all its rivals had modern overhead-valve V-8s, Packard's famously smooth but increasingly antiquated flathead straight eight was beginning to be a detriment to sales—which indeed dropped significantly for '52.

Left: Only Packard's 250 series included a Mayfair hardtop—a stunner when two-toned. Ultramatic added $189 to its $3318 price. Power came from Packard's 327-cubic-inch straight-eight, offered since 1948. Mated to Ultramatic, it produced 155 horsepower; with stick shift, 150.

Above: The 250 series consisted of just two body styles, both available only in this series. The 250 Mayfair hardtop coupe and 250 convertible were priced at $3318 and $3476, respectively, and together accounted for a mere 5200 sales. By far the biggest seller was Packard's entry-level 200 series, but the popularity of these midpriced cars only served to further dilute the company's luxury image.

Small hoods tacked over the top of the taillights identified '52 Studebakers from the rear, but the real change was up front. Gone was the popular but controversial bullet-nose, replaced by a low, wide, "toothy" grille that prompted the nickname "clam digger."

An ad stresses the "Jet-streamed styling and standout gas saving" of the 1952 models. A Commander convertible was given center stage, but in the lower right corner was pictured a '52 newcomer: the Starliner hardtop coupe, which was offered in the Champion and Commander lines. The former cost $2220, the latter $2488, both about $280 more than the conventional coupes.

A Commander convertible paced the 1952 running of the Indianapolis 500, the only time during the decade an independent automaker was given that honor. It was a fitting way to celebrate Studebaker's 100th anniversary.

A stately 1952 Commander sedan shows off its chrome-trimmed instrument panel and "suicide" rear doors—so named because with the car parked at the curb, passengers exiting the street-side rear seat risked being crushed by the door if it was struck by a vehicle coming from behind. Whitewall tires and the wing-shaped front bumper guard were options. Commander sedans were offered in Regal or State trim, priced at $2121 and $2208, respectively.

Above: Hardtop styling came to Studebaker for 1952. This Commander Starliner has a 232-cid V-8 under its sloped hood. The firm marked its centennial in '52.

Left: Workaday Champion with the new divided grille.

1953

Voracious as Americans were becoming in their quest for consumer goods, they couldn't—and wouldn't—buy everything on the market. Dismayed at slackening car sales, the Big Three automakers pondered ways to rekindle interest in their wares. The folks at Ford thought they had the answer: send scads of new cars to dealers, and let them discover ways to dispose of the glut. Chevrolet followed suit with its own retailers.

Thus began the sales blitz of 1953-54, a period of flamboyant promotions, high-pressure tactics, and frenzied dealers—an age of excess that set the stage for government action later in the decade. Production controls had been lifted in February, as Dwight Eisenhower took the presidency from Harry Truman, so showrooms ballooned with unordered vehicles.

Buicks, Chevrolets, and Pontiacs got new squared-up silhouettes. So did all four Chrysler products. Ford stood pat, for the most part, with the restyled bodies that had arrived a year earlier. Stunner of the season, though, was the new Studebaker coupe—a milestone design that

nevertheless failed to reverse the company's failing fortunes.

Having fallen in love with styling, Americans were easy prey to hard-sell techniques—especially since those luscious hardtops and roomy wagons could be bought on "easy" time payments. Delayed gratification—postponing purchases until cash was at hand—was a vestige of the past, not a theme for the prosperous present, much less the future. In the increasingly status-conscious suburbs, people began to define their personalities by their possessions. Owning a big, fully loaded car, suggested some psychologists, allowed a person to feel more significant.

It took an average of 30 weeks' work to buy a new car, as opposed to 37 weeks back in 1925—before the 1930s Depression. Bread cost 16 cents a pound in 1953, round steak 92 cents. Eggs were 70 cents a dozen, coffee 89 cents a pound. Traveling coast-to-coast (one-way) cost almost $57 on a Greyhound bus, or $99 via TWA. An off-brand air conditioner went for $289 at Macy's, while a new Buick Special ran $2197 and Chevrolets started at $1524.

With wage and price controls halted, and unemployment dipping to just 2.9 percent, median family income edged past $4200. Workers earned an average of $3581 annually. The average employee grossed $64 a week at his $1.61 hourly rate. Auto workers made $88 per week. Teachers collected an average $4254 per year. Workers looked forward to ever-increasing prosperity and an ever-expanding number of consumer goods.

TV viewers got to see Steve Allen on *The Tonight Show*, and Danny Thomas in *Make Room for Daddy*. Bob Hope hosted the first Academy Awards show on TV. Mary Martin and Ethel Merman celebrated Ford's 50th anniversary on CBS and NBC. Frank Sinatra revived his flagging career in the role of Maggio in *From Here to Eternity*, which was named best picture. Alan Ladd and Jack Palance dueled in the saloon in *Shane*. Three-D movies appeared, but the use of special viewing glasses limited their popularity.

Tony Bennett sang "Rags to Riches," and Patti Page warbled about a "Doggie in the Window." Hugh Hefner launched *Playboy* magazine in Chicago, and *TV Guide* appeared on newsstands. The first successful open-heart surgery was performed—and a young Elvis Presley paid four bucks to cut a record to celebrate his mother's birthday.

Americans spoke derisively of intellectuals as "eggheads," a term applied to Adlai Stevenson in his losing battle for the presidency in '52. Former GM chief "Engine Charlie" Wilson, named secretary of defense in the new Administration, uttered one of the most noted phrases of the decade: "What was good for our country was good for General Motors and vice versa." Mildly misquoted in the present tense, the seemingly arrogant assertion drew flak for years to come.

As the Korean War ended on July 26, 1953, most Americans gazed avidly forward, foreseeing even greater prosperity for themselves and the nation. The average motorist drove 10,000 miles yearly—a figure that's remained surprisingly steady. Who wanted to pile up those miles in an old clunker—or a stripped-down Ford Mainline or Chevrolet One-Fifty—when a host of more inviting choices beckoned?

Chrysler Corporation

All Chryslers received a one-piece windshield for 1953. Air conditioning was newly optional, joined late in the model year by Chrysler's first automatic transmission, the two-speed PowerFlite. Just over 2500 New Yorker Newport hardtop coupes were sold at $3487.

Conspicuous by its absence from this ad is the performance-oriented midline Saratoga, which was dropped for 1953; oddly, the name would reappear a few years later. Imperial isn't mentioned either, but it remained in the lineup.

Above: Though Chrysler was best known for its powerful Hemi V-8, the make's biggest seller for 1953 was the six-cylinder Windsor series. And the best-selling Windsor was the $2691 Deluxe four-door sedan.

Below: Imperials sat on a longer wheelbase than Windsor and New Yorker, giving them a distinctive—and distinguished—look. The $4225 four-door sedan was the most popular, yet sold only 7800 copies.

DeSoto again showed a toothy grille for 1953. Like all Chrysler Corp. cars, it got a one-piece windshield; unlike some of the others (Dodge and Plymouth), it benefited from optional air conditioning. Six-cylinder models were called Powermasters, V-8s were Firedomes.

This $3114 Firedome convertible sports the wire wheels that were offered on all Chrysler Corp. cars for '53.

Above: Engineering advancements tended to trickle down the corporate ladder, and, for 1953, the Hemi V-8 trickled down to Dodge. Predictably, it was smaller than those fitted to Chryslers and DeSotos. Called the Red Ram, it displaced 241 cubic inches and made 140 horsepower. What hadn't yet trickled down was an automatic transmission; the best Dodge could offer was its semiautomatic Gyro-Torque Drive, a variation of Fluid Drive.

Left: Along with the V-8 came a new model name: Coronet. It also brought a new ram's-head hood ornament, which would be revived during the 1980s for the company's trucks. The only convertible offered was the $2494 Coronet.

Plymouth offered only two-door station wagons by this time, four-door versions having been dropped after 1950. They were available in both Plymouth lines for that year: the Cambridge ($2064) and dressier Cranbrook ($2207).

Above: Though it wore a one-piece windshield and optional wire wheels for 1953 like its corporate brothers, bottom-rung Plymouth had yet to get a V-8—or even a semiautomatic transmission. That put it at a disadvantage in the low-price field, so late in the model year, Plymouth finally got a version of Fluid Drive called Hy-Drive. By far the best seller of the line was the $1873 Cranbrook four-door sedan.

Below: Though the lowly Plymouth nameplate may have seemed out of place at a ritzy ski lodge, a dressy Cranbrook Belvedere two-door hardtop didn't—and it cost just $2064.

Most expensive of all Plymouths for '53 was the $2220 Cranbrook convertible. All Plymouths were powered by the same 217-cubic-inch flathead six used since '42, but it now put out a rousing 100 horsepower.

Ford Motor Company

Above: Crestline buyers could opt for a sporty Victoria hardtop at $1941. "Vicky" hardtops got a new one-piece backlight. The grille and side trim were revised.

Fords were treated to a mild facelift for 1953, which would turn out to be the final year for the venerable flathead V-8. And that's what powers this Crestline Sunliner convertible, which started at $2043.

Below: Ford was putting on a full-court sales press in an effort to catch Chevrolet (it didn't work), and this ad attempted to convey the wisdom in buying two.

This midline $1582 Customline two-door sedan also sports the V-8, which was good for 110 horsepower in its final year.

Only subtle styling changes marked the 1953 Lincolns in a year that brought big changes underhood: Engineers found another 45 horses hiding in the 317-cubic-inch V-8, which now corralled a total of 205. All those ponies could be enjoyed in a Cosmopolitan hardtop for $3322.

This brochure cover shows one of the multicolor interiors available in a Lincoln.

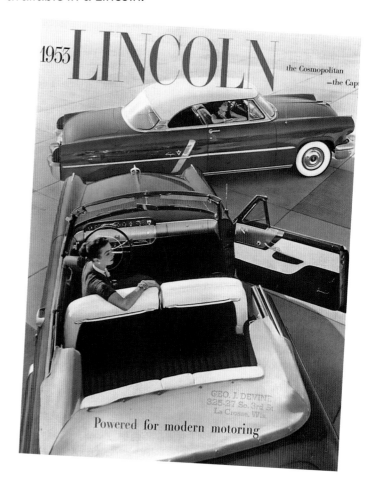

Above: Unbelievably, it happened again. For the second year in a row, Lincolns placed 1-2-3-4 in the *Carrera Panamericana* road race.

Left: Engines of Lincolns in the Mexican race were fitted with Champion spark plugs. Naturally, Champion suggested that owners of other cars might expect similar performance.

The line was now divided into Custom and top-line Monterey models, the latter hosting this $2390 convertible.

Indeed, one had to "Take a good look" to see any changes in the '53 Mercurys, which received little more than trim revisions.

Above: Outside visors were fading out of popularity, but the Monterey sedan—with standard skirts and two-toning—attracted a healthy share of customers. A Monterey sedan went for $2133.

Below: Henry the Deuce, Benson, and William Clay Ford pose with the 40-millionth Ford vehicle, a Mercury Monterey convertible, during Ford's 50th-anniversary year.

The outrageously priced woody wagons were in their final year; subsequent wagons would be less expensive all-steel versions.

A Roadmaster convertible tipped the price scale at $3506.

Above: Buicks received a number of changes for 1953 to celebrate the division's 50th anniversary. Freshened styling was punctuated by twin bullet taillights, and while entry-level Specials retained a 263-cubic-inch inline eight, Supers and Roadmasters got a new 322-cid overhead-valve V-8 making 188 horsepower.

Below: The fabulous Buick Skylark was a limited-production, convertible-only car that, like the Olds Fiesta and Cadillac Eldorado, began life on the show circuit. Skylark sold better for '53 than the other two combined, and helped cement Buick's status as GM's near-luxury make. It featured a cut-down windshield and lower silhouette, along with rounded wheelwell cutouts and standard wire wheels, and would define the division's styling through 1957.

Left: GM introduced a striking trio of specialty convertibles for 1953. Buick's was the stunning—and stunningly expensive—Skylark. At $5000, it cost $1500 more than a similar Roadmaster. Only 1690 were built, one reason these gorgeous cars are such coveted classics today.

Cadillac's version of GM's 1953 specialty convertibles introduced the now-famous Eldorado moniker. Those who thought Buick's Skylark was expensive would be floored by the whopping $7750 sticker on the Eldo—which didn't look that much different than a $4144 Series 62 ragtop. Only 532 buyers ponied up the bucks.

Above: Minor styling changes marked the regular '53 Caddys, whose 331-cubic-inch V-8 now put out 210 horsepower. Shown is the $3995 Coupe de Ville.

Below: What started as a 1953 Motorama show car went on sale a scant six months later as the legendary Corvette. Unfortunately, its mechanical components couldn't support the promise made by its racy, two-seat fiberglass body. Beneath the hood was Chevy's aging 235-cubic-inch six, and though boosted from 115 horse-power to 150 for this application, it was backed by the company's Powerglide two-speed automatic transmission—a scourge to sports-car purists, who preferred manual transmissions. Priced at a stiff $3515, production was limited to just 315 units—all of them Polo White with red interiors.

Eldorados sported a wraparound windshield and a color-keyed metal top boot.

Riding a four-inch-longer wheelbase than the Series 62s was the lone Series Sixty Special four-door sedan priced at $4305.

More palatable to 1953 ragtop fans was the top-line Bel Air convertible at $2175.

Above: Rounding out the trio of GM's 1953 specialty convertibles was Oldsmobile's flashy Fiesta. It carried unique "spinner" wheelcovers, knockoffs of which became widely favored by customizers. Less popular was the car itself: at a lofty $5717, it fell between the Buick Skylark and Cadillac Eldorado in price, and didn't match the sales of either. Just 458 found buyers.

Below: This Ninety-Eight Holiday coupe wears fashionable wire wheels and shows the division's signature bullet taillights.

Considering Chevy was a low-price make, it's surprising that the flashy $1874 Bel Air sedan sold nearly a quarter-million copies.

Oldsmobiles earned some styling changes for 1953. They were most noticeable on the 88, which now had a similar tail treatment to the Ninety-Eight. Elliptical pods atop the canted bumper guards would become a familiar Olds shape during the next few years, showing up on grilles and taillights.

Dependability may have been a solid selling point in 1953, but it was a long way from the performance image Pontiac would push later in the decade.

A rare hauler is this sedan delivery, with its blanked-out rear side windows.

Above: Pontiacs were treated to a longer wheelbase and major reskin for '53. A one-piece windshield appeared, along with kicked-up rear fenders.

Left: Extra chrome was added as well, as evidenced by this $2446 Chieftain Eight Custom Catalina hardtop. Eights only cost about $75 more than comparable Sixes, and for good reason: When GM's Hydra-Matic automatic transmission was ordered—which was about 75 percent of the time—the six-cylinder engine now put out 118 horsepower, while the eight remained at 122. Newly optional for '53 was power steering.

Hudson Motor Car Corporation

Above: Hudson simplified its model lineup for 1953. What had been the Pacemaker took on the Wasp name, the former Wasp became the Super Wasp, and the Hornet became the lone long-wheelbase flagship, as the equally priced Commodore Eight was dropped. Shown is a Super Wasp in two-door sedan form, a body style not offered in Hornet trim.

Right: The economy-priced Hudson Jet debuted following a $12 million development program. Jets rode a 105-inch wheelbase, carried a 202-cid engine, and employed the same Monobilt construction as large Hudsons. Despite Rambler's success, Jet sales failed to take off. In addition to its price, the ultimate failure of the Jet was also attributed to its slab-sided styling.

In an effort to duplicate Nash's success with the compact Rambler, Hudson brought out the compact Jet for 1953. Unfortunately, sales never took off. Part of the problem was the car's tall, ungainly look, and part was the price: The cheapest Jet cost $1858—nearly $200 more than a base full-size Chevrolet—and this better-trimmed Super Jet four-door sedan listed for $1954. All Jets were powered by a 202-cubic-inch six. Developing the Jet cost a bundle that Hudson couldn't afford to lose, and the car's failure likely forced the company's merger with Nash.

Kaiser-Frazer Corporation

A 1953 Henry J shows off the facelift it got for '52. Also added at that time was a trunklid, which was previously absent. Prices now ranged from $1399 to $1561. Some unsold 1953 models were reserialed and sold as '54s, after which the Henry J was put out to pasture.

A '53 Corsair with a cleaner grille, vertical Cadillac-like taillamps, and back-up lights.

Above: Dragon trim was revived for a 1953 Kaiser of the same name, which listed for a pricey $3924. It wore gold-plated ornamentation along with a padded top and distinct interior materials.

Left: More reasonable was the '53 Kaiser Deluxe Traveler at $2619.

Nash Motors

Above: Ramblers got a squared-up front end for 1953 that made them more closely resemble their bigger brothers. Two new six-cylinder engines were offered: an 85-horsepower 184-cubic-inch version with manual transmission, and a 90-hp 195-cid with automatic. This convertible topped the range at $2150.

Right: Statesman's engine was bumped to 100 hp for '53, when this two-door Super sold for $2143.

Left: Nash ads promoted the '53 Statesman and Ambassador as "Pinin Farina's latest styling triumph," but in fact, they were little-changed in appearance from 1952. What was new was optional power steering and a dual-carbureted version of the Ambassador's 252-cubic-inch six, which added 20 horsepower for a total of 140.

Below: A LeMans coupe version of the Nash-Healey was added for 1953. It rode a longer wheelbase than the convertible and was priced even higher: $6399 vs. $5908. Nash's story would continue under American Motors Corporation, which was formed when the company merged with Hudson in early 1954.

Packard Motor Car Corporation

Packard tried to differentiate its high-priced cars from the midpriced lines for 1953 by renaming the latter Clipper and Clipper Deluxe; the bigger cars were now Cavalier and Patrician.

Richard Arbib's '52 Pan American show car led to the 1953 Caribbean, which sported open wheel wells, a hood scoop, and wire wheels

Above: New for '53 was the elaborately decorated—and astronomically priced—Caribbean convertible. Among its identifying touches were radiused wheelwells heavily outlined in chrome, wire wheels, and a lack of side trim. Competing directly against similar specialty convertibles from General Motors, the Caribbean sold just 750 copies, but that was enough to beat Cadillac's Eldorado. Newly available on upper-line Packards was the Caribbean's new 180-horsepower version of the 327 straight eight.

Left: Twice as many people bought a conventional $3486 Packard convertible as purchased the high-price Caribbean, thereby saving themselves $1724.

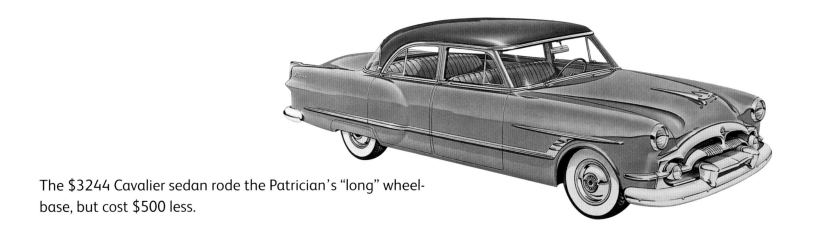

The $3244 Cavalier sedan rode the Patrician's "long" wheelbase, but cost $500 less.

Newly available on the $3278 Mayfair hardtop was an "outside spare" continental kit.

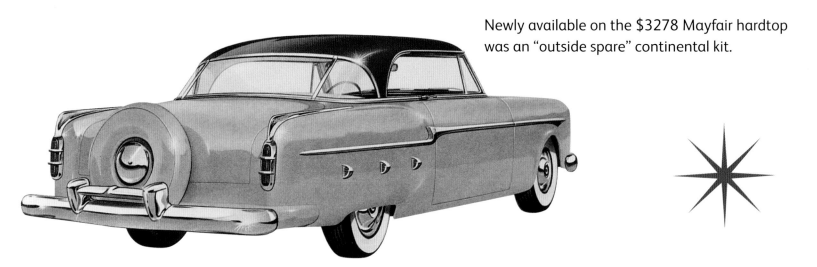

Packard's cheapest car for 1953 was the $2544 Clipper club sedan. Priced in Buick/Chrysler/Oldsmobile territory, Clippers accounted for the bulk of Packard sales.

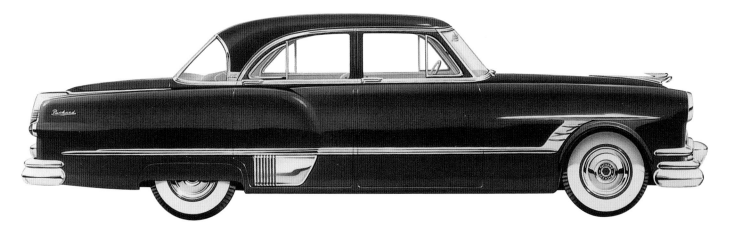

At the other end of the spectrum was the $3740 Patrician sedan, which cost about the same as a Cadillac but sold in far lower volume. Packard sales were reasonably healthy—as was the company's financial status—when it merged with (actually bought) Studebaker in 1954, thereby forming the Studebaker-Packard Corporation.

Finlike fender trim was new to the Patrician, which topped the '53 senior line.

Studebaker Corporation

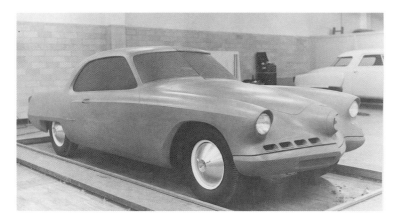

Left: In late 1950, during the ultimately doomed effort to design the Model N, Raymond Loewy decided he wanted a show car. Loewy gave four teams of his stylists 10 days to come up with something. The winning design was a coupe from Bob Bourke that was so striking that Studebaker couldn't resist putting a version of it into production for 1953.

Below: Studebakers were redesigned for 1953, with straight-through rear fenders and a sloped nose. Four-door models abandoned their suicide rear doors for conventional ones, as shown on this Land Cruiser, which remained the top-line sedan and again rode a longer wheelbase—now 120.5 inches.

Above: Sharing the Land Cruiser's stretched chassis were rakish new Starlight pillared coupes. Whether in six-cylinder Champion or V-8 Commander guise, their long, low silhouette and smooth lines put them light-years ahead of other American cars in terms of styling.

Right: No '53 car deserved the Fashion Academy Award more than Studebaker. As *Motor World* reported, Studebaker "made every other American car look ten years older."

Six-cylinder Champion and V-8 Commander sedans now sat on the same 116.5-inch wheelbase.

The new American car with the European look!

THE NEW
1953 STUDEBAKER

Even sleeker than the Starlight pillared coupe was the Starliner hardtop coupe. Starliners cost $161 more than Starlights and were likewise offered in both the Champion and Commander lines. As a Champion with the 85-horsepower 169-cubic-inch six, it went for $2116, while in Commander form with the 120-hp 232-cid V-8, it listed for $2374—making it Studebaker's most expensive model. Shown is the Commander Starliner, with V-8 badges on its hood, rear flanks, and trunklid. The rear view shows the oblong vertical taillights fitted to all '53 Studebakers. Whether in pillared or hardtop form, these beautiful cars are often referred to as the "Loewy coupes," after Studebaker's head of styling, Raymond Loewy. But they were actually the work of Bob Bourke, who had also penned Studebaker's 1950 bullet-nose models. But as coveted as these cars are today, they didn't help Studebaker's plight much in 1953. Sales had been steadily dropping since 1950's high of 320,000, and by this time, they were less than half that. And due to productivity problems at Studebaker's high-overhead South Bend, Indiana, plant, the company needed to build 250,000 cars a year just to break even. Three steady years of red ink with no color change in sight forced Studebaker to seek a savior, and found it in Packard Corporation. The two merged in 1954 to form the Studebaker-Packard Corporation, where the story of both marques continued.

1954

As car dealers struggled to recover from the impact of the sales blitz that began in 1952, Ford and Chevrolet accountants tallied their sales totals. Some critics decried the high-pressure tactics and carnival-like atmosphere that had prevailed. A modest outcry emerged against misleading ads and shady practices. Meanwhile, consumers began to hold back on purchases. Every make except Oldsmobile showed a production slump in the '54 model year.

The biggest losers were the independent makes, facing the opening salvo of a shakeout that was destined to thin their ranks. Nash took over an ailing Hudson company in the spring. Then, in autumn, Studebaker and Packard merged into one—neither firm having been on solid financial footing. Kaiser was about to disappear. A U.S. congressman even charged that Ford and GM were trying to monopolize the industry and called for a full-scale investigation.

Except for a cute little British-built Metropolitan from Nash, a short-lived Kaiser-Darrin roadster, and a reappearance of the Century in Buick's lineup, there was little in the way of model shuffling or new introductions in '54. Under the hoods, however, existing engines grew stronger and the overhead-valve V-8 increased its foothold in the market. In all, 15 out of the 18 car makes announced higher engine outputs.

Ford launched a pair of new Y-block V-8 engines, elbowing aside the long-lived flathead design. Chrysler's hottest Hemi leaped to 235 horsepower. Oldsmobile's V-8 grew bigger. Packard had no V-8, but enlarged its long-familiar straight-eight to mammoth dimensions. Pontiac made do with its L-head inline eight for another season—but everyone knew a modern V-8 was waiting in the wings.

Big General Motors cars adopted Panoramic windshields, setting a trend for the decade. Packard took the lead with tubeless tires—soon to become standard across the industry. Chrysler tucked a gas turbine engine into a Plymouth Belvedere.

A recession that stretched from 1953 into '54 subsided quickly—and completely. Unemployment reached 5.5 percent—well above the 1953 figure—though inflation remained modest, and the economy in general continued to grow.

Millions of Americans looked forward to a ranch home in the suburbs, with one (or more) cars in the garage—plus shorter work hours to allow more leisure time. As more wives entered the labor force, families also grew to expect more in terms of education, nutrition, and medical services.

Workers were encouraged—by advertising and by fellow employees—to buy the American dream for "no money down." Even youngsters were rapidly absorbed into the blossoming consumer society, led down that path by both peers and parents.

"The average American male," declared *Reader's Digest*, "thinks the ability to run a home smoothly and efficiently is the most important quality in a wife." In that vein, *Father Knows Best* premiered on TV, starring Robert Young as the "perfect" Dad. Color sets went on the market, but programs still aired in black-and-white. Smiling pianist Liberace attracted a wide female audience on TV. Senator Joe McCarthy initiated the Army-McCarthy hearings—also attracting a sizable share of television viewers.

Willie Mays led the National League in hitting with a .345 average, Bill Vukovich won the Indy 500 for the second year in a row, and Englishman Roger Bannister was the first man to run a mile in under four minutes. Children began to receive Salk polio vaccine, Boeing tested the first 707 jet, and the first atomic-powered submarine was commissioned.

A trend toward do-it-yourself projects began to develop—including maintenance tasks on the family automobile. Gasoline cost about 29 cents a gallon—equivalent to $1.30 or so in today's currency.

William Littlewood, president of the Society of Automotive Engineers, decried the lack of focus on safety, insisting that the horsepower race "isn't engineering—it's a fight between sales forces." Of the million vehicles participating in a Check Your Car program, one-fourth flunked the safety test.

Like it or not, the die was cast. Nearly every automaker planned to play engine-performance leapfrog by '55, as the remaining members of the Big Three—and newly merged independents—readied new bodies and small-block V-8 engines.

American Motors Corporation

It was a financial shotgun wedding that brought longtime manufacturers Hudson and Nash together in 1954 to form American Motors Corporation.

Hudson was the older of the two marques, having been established in 1909, nearly a decade before the first Nash appeared. Hudson had long been a midprice make with an accent on performance, a reputation that blossomed during the early Fifties with the potent Hornet.

Nash was known more for its stout construction, practicality, and operating economy. It was one of the first companies to introduce true unitized construction, and later set itself apart with its sleek "bathtub" styling.

After the postwar seller's boom subsided in the early 1950s, both companies found themselves being squeezed by the full-court sales press being applied by the Big Three—Ford Motor Co., General Motors, and Chrysler Corporation. Both Nash and Hudson turned to compacts as a means to provide choices the Big Three didn't.

Top executives of the newly formed American Motors Corporation were (from left to right) Abraham E. Barit of Hudson, George W. Mason of Nash, and fellow Nash exec George Romney. Mason was named president of AMC, soon to be succeeded by Romney.

Hudson's Hornet was powered by a potent 308-cubic-inch flathead six that helped make it a stock-car-racing hero. Also contributing was its Step-down design, which placed the body between the Monobilt frame rails, thus lowering the center of gravity for better handling.

Right: As indicated by its trunklid badge, this 1954 Hornet club coupe is powered by Hudson's hot Twin H-Power six with twin carburetors and a mighty 170 horsepower. A special 7-X racing version reportedly put out close to 220 hp. Hudson's lower-priced Wasp looked like the Hornet, but was shorter and carried a smaller engine.

Below: A Hornet Brougham convertible topped the regular Hudson line at $3288.

Hornet's big four-door sedan carried a long, sloping roofline and a $2769 price tag.

Above: At the opposite end of the 1954 spectrum was the compact Jet, with a 202-cid six. A flashy $2057 Jet Liner sedan is shown, but other models started as low as $1621.

Right: Built in Italy with an aluminum body atop a Jet chassis, the exotic Hudson Italia cost an equally exotic $4800—and sold just 26 copies.

Above: If Hudson was known as a racetrack demon, Nash was known as a mobile motel. This ad mentions the fact that a Nash's seats could be folded down to form a bed. But by 1954, nearly everyone already knew it. No father ever wanted to see his daughter's date arrive in a Nash.

Below: With no convertible in the line, the $2735 Ambassador Custom Country Club coupe was the most expensive "regular" '54 Nash. With Nash's conservative image, it's no wonder it was outsold by its sedan counterpart by a 16-to-1 margin.

The company's top 1954 sedan was the $2600 Ambassador Custom. Power for the big Ambassadors came from a 252-cubic-inch six with 140 horsepower. A midprice line, the Statesman, shared the Ambassador's styling, but was shorter in length and powered by a smaller 100-hp six.

Nash had its own exotic in the Italian-designed, British-built Nash-Healey. A convertible version was dropped for 1954, leaving a $6000 coupe that sold fewer than 100 copies before being discontinued itself.

A new addition to the Nash family was the baby Metropolitan. Imported from England, it carried a 74-cubic-inch four-cylinder engine boasting 42 horsepower—and great fuel economy. The coupe version cost $1445, the convertible just $1469.

Cheerfully hued Metropolitans had enclosed front wheels resulting in a large turning radius—typical of Nashes—along with a jaunty spare tire out back. Three-passenger capacity was declared, but only two folks fit easily.

Above: The most popular boat in Nash's fleet was the compact Rambler, sales of which probably kept the company afloat during these years. A surprising number of body styles were offered, including a two-door hardtop and a unique semiconvertible, actually a two-door sedan with a full fold-back fabric roof. Standard engine was a 185-cid 85-hp six, though a 90-hp six was also offered. Prices ranged from $1550 to $2050.

Below: In addition to the usual two doors (shown), a top-of-the-line four-door Rambler Custom Cross Country station wagon went on sale, on a longer wheelbase.

Chrysler Corporation

Revisions to the grille and headlight bezels gave Chryslers a fresh face for 1954. Horsepower of the Hemi V-8, still at 331 cubic inches, rose from 180 to 195 in New Yorker, and went to 235 in New Yorker Deluxe and Imperial. A flashy New Yorker Deluxe convertible cost a princely $3938.

The Beautiful Chrysler WINDSOR DELUXE

THE BIG CAR IN THE MEDIUM PRICE FIELD

Left: Windsor was still powered by a 264-cid six with 119 hp, but not for long; this would prove to be the final year for that combination. Windsor prices started at about $2550.

Below: A Town & Country wagon was offered in both the Windsor and New Yorker lines. This New Yorker version cost a sobering $4024—and had predictably low sales.

Listing for well above that was the $4560 Custom Imperial Newport hardtop coupe.

A special-edition DeSoto Coronado boasted extra chrome trim and dressy interior.

Availability of Chrysler Corporation's two-speed PowerFlite automatic transmission was expanded to the lesser lines for 1954, making it an option for this Hemi-powered DeSoto Firedome Sportsman hardtop coupe.

Dodge's lightweight, Hemi-powered cars were quite successful in racing, and a Royal 500 convertible paced the Indy 500 that year. To capitalize on this honor, Dodge released 701 replicas. Factory options included Power-Flite automatic transmission for $189, power steering for $134, and Airtemp air conditioning for $643. A grille divider would be a Dodge feature for the next few years.

Above: Royal was added as Dodge's new top-line series for 1954. Low-line Meadowbrook and midline Coronet were available with either a 110-horsepower six or a 140-hp Hemi V-8, but the Royal was V-8 only. This $2503 Royal hardtop displays a distinctive two-tone paint scheme that was predictive of what would arrive for '55.

Right: It wasn't until midway through the 1954 model year that Plymouth finally got an automatic-transmission option—Chrysler's two-speed PowerFlite—a feature that rival Chevrolet had offered since 1950. Also arriving midyear was a larger 230-cubic-inch six with 10 more horsepower, now 110. New model names graced a lineup that otherwise saw only detail changes. Topping the range was the Belvedere, a moniker previously worn by a lone hardtop coupe. This Belvedere convertible was the most expensive Plymouth at $2301.

Unlike the lower-line Plaza and Savoy, all Belvederes except the wagon wore little tacked-on chrome tailfins. The four-door sedan went for $1953.

Belvedere sport coupes shared the two-tone beltline dip of the convertibles. This version also wears optional wire wheels and continental kit.

Note the exposed tailgate hinges on the finless $2288 Belvedere Suburban two-door wagon.

Ford Motor Company

In a year that brought few styling changes of note, Ford redefined the sunroof concept for 1954 with the Crestline Skyliner. Traditional sunroofs—as they're known today—first appeared in the late 1930s, but the Skyliner took a different approach: The whole forward half of the roof was made of tinted glass, and yes, it tended to bake the interior in sunny climates. This model was offered only in the top-line Crestline series for $2164, a $109 price premium over a standard Victoria hardtop.

The biggest change to the 1954 Ford appeared under the hood: After 20 years of faithful service, the flathead V-8 was finally put out to pasture. In its place was a new Y-Block overhead-valve V-8 of the same displacement: 239 cubic inches. As testimony to the added efficiency of the new design, horsepower rose from 110 to 130.

Lincolns likewise looked little different for 1954, and could boast of neither new models nor more power. A total of 13,598 Capri four-door sedans rolled off the line—highest sedan production figure in the 1952-55 era. This year's cost: $3711.

Mercury offered its own glass-roof model for 1956, the $2582 Monterey Sun Valley. In addition to making scenery more viewable, the see-through roof was good for overhead traffic lights—and provided the same weather protection as a solid-steel top. Just 9761 were built, selling for $2582 ($130 more than a plain hardtop).

Above: Mercury claimed interior temperatures in a Sun Valley rose only five degrees in direct sunlight, but some disgruntled owners complained of stifling heat. A zip-in vinyl cover kept the sun out completely. Sun Valleys had special interior trim combinations and body color schemes.

Left: Mercury styling changes were minimal for '56, but available as an option were bullet front-bumper guards, as shown on this $2610 Monterey convertible.

Below: The least expensive '54 Mercury, a $2194 Custom two-door sedan, is shown wearing the standard front bumper.

General Motors

The exotic Skylark specialty convertible returned for 1954, but this time, it was just a little less special. It was also a little less expensive: $4483 versus the $5000 asked for the '53 version. It was essentially a standard convertible with shaved port-holes, sloping trunklid, and unique taillights.

The Skylark's resemblance to a $2964 Super convertible is obvious. All Buicks got larger, "squarer" bodies for '54, along with wraparound windshields.

The surviving straight-eight engine in the Special was axed, replaced by a 264-cubic-inch 150-horsepower version of the upper models' 322-cid V-8, which added ponies for '54: up to 200 in the top-line Roadmaster. That engine was also offered in a new "hot rod" Buick (seemingly a contradiction) called the Century. Actually, the name—and the concept—weren't new. Before World War II, a Century carried Buick's biggest engine in a midsize body, and was named for its ability to hit 100 mph right off the showroom floor. For 1954, it was offered in coupe, convertible, and sedan forms, along with this unlikely station wagon, which listed for $3470.

Left: Like Buicks, Cadillacs got squared-up bodies for 1954 along with a new front-end treatment. Wheelbases grew by three inches, and the 331 V-8 produced 20 more horsepower, now 230. By far the most popular Cadillac was this $3933 Series 62 sedan.

Below: Like its Buick Skylark counterpart, the specialty Eldorado convertible returned for '54, also ending up a closer relation to other cars in the line. This was reflected in a price cut of more than $2000, putting it at a "mere" $5738. A regular Series 62 convertible cost $1300 less.

Chevys got a mild facelift for 1954, and their 235-cubic-inch six gained 10 horsepower, for a top rating of 125.

Joining the "squarer body brigade" led by Buick and Cadillac, 1954 Oldsmobiles boasted a much sleeker, more modern look. All models gained two inches in wheelbase, and engine size increased from 303 cubic inches to 324. That brought 185 horses to the Super 88 corral. A Holiday coupe cost $2688, a convertible, $2868.

Corvette color choices quadrupled with the addition of blue, red, and black to the carry-over white. Production increased more than tenfold to 3640.

A Super 88 convertible shows off the new thinner bright trim for the upper grille.

Right: Replacing the slow-selling Fiesta specialty convertible was the new Starfire, likewise offered only in ragtop form. It was essentially the top-line Ninety-Eight convertible with a fancy name and special trim. It was easily distinguishable by its "spectacular sweep-cut rear fenders"—meaning the wheel well cutouts. It listed for $3276, about the same as the previous Ninety-Eight convertible, and oceans less than the $5717 Fiesta.

Below: Sharing the Starfire's spectacular fenders was the $2826 Ninety-Eight Holiday hardtop coupe. Ninety-Eight sedans didn't get the feature.

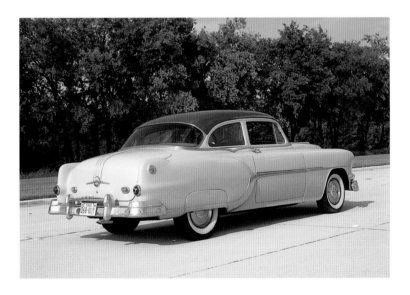

A Chieftain Six two-door sedan was the cheapest Pontiac at $1968.

Left: A new top-line Pontiac arrived for 1954 with a longer wheelbase than other models. Called the Star Chief, it featured extended rear quarter panels and unique trim. Prices ran about $100 more than comparable Chieftain Eights. This Star Chief Catalina hardtop listed for $2557.

Below: Since Pontiacs received only minor trim changes for 1954, they looked a bit dated next to their rebodied Buick and Olds counterparts. They also cost a bit more: In two-door hardtop form, this $2458 Chieftain Eight Custom Catalina was $153 more than a Buick Special, $9 more than an Olds 88.

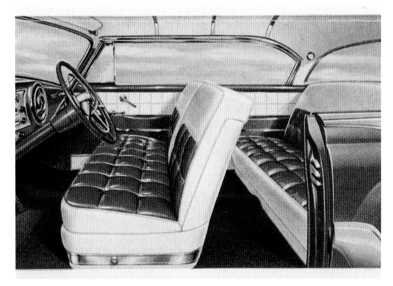

Kaiser-Willys Corporation

Above: Styling studio head Arnott "Buzz" Grisinger with a mock-up of his facelift for the 1954 Kaiser, circa 1951. The concave grille and oval headlamp housings were copied from the Buick XP-300 show car that company president Edgar Kaiser admired. Grisinger added a hood scoop and bold canted bumper guards. Cost issues toned down the latter, though.

Below: Grisinger soon went out on his own, but still provided ideas to Kaiser. Bob Gurr, a young designer who had recently quit Ford, was recruited to come up with more sketches for Grisinger for possible updates.

In 1952, designer Dutch Darrin spent his own money to design a sports car of glass-reinforced plastic to ride the Henry J chassis. Introduced as a '54 model, the Kaiser-Darrin (so named by Henry Kaiser) had a three-way folding top with an available fiberglass hardtop, a medallion-like grille piece above a concave nose section, a long hood, tapering rear quarters, and teardrop taillights adapted from standard '52 Kaiser units. A handful were super-charged. Considerable interest was generated by the doors, which slid forward electrically on rollers. They didn't slide forward quite far enough, though, making entry and exit a chore. Before the flaw could be addressed, production of the rakish Kaiser-Darrin was suspended.

Despite its financial problems, the company produced a handful of fiberglass-bodied Kaiser-Darrin sports cars for 1954. Using leftover chassis and 90-horsepower six-cylinder engines from the departed Henry J, it had a novel sliding side door and a steep $3668 price, which attracted only 435 buyers.

Kaisers received a facelift for 1954, and top-line Manhattans got a 140-hp supercharged version of the 226-cubic-inch six. This four-door version carried a $2670 price tag.

The entry-level '54 was the handsome Special. Early versions lacked the wraparound backlight.

Still believing in the viability of compact cars, Henry J. Kaiser bought Willys-Overland in 1954, which got him the little Willys Aero. The Aero was larger than the Henry J but also more expensive; the cheapest four-cylinder Aero Lark (shown) cost $1737, which could easily buy a larger six-cylinder Chevrolet. Aero also offered a six-cylinder engine—two actually: a 191-cubic-inch Willys with 90 horsepower, and Kaiser's own 226-cid with 115 hp.

Studebaker-Packard Corporation

Thanks to the success of its redesigned 1951 models, Packard was on fairly sound financial footing when it purchased moribund Studebaker in 1954. The Studebaker-Packard buyout was supposed to be a prelude to a Studebaker-Packard-Hudson-Nash merger intended to create a ladder-type corporation to rival Chrysler Corp., Ford Motor Co., and General Motors—thereby turning the Big Three into the Big Four. Unfortunately, Studebaker's many woes were not fully understood at the time of the buyout, and the flailing company pushed Packard ahead of it down the slippery slope to ruin.

Right: Packard had introduced the Clipper name in 1953 to denote its midpriced offerings, and they were by far the best-selling models. Topping the 1954 range was the $3125 Clipper Super Panama hardtop coupe, but other Clippers started as low as $2544. Clippers were identified by a unique tail treatment and slightly different grille. Depending on model, they packed either a 288-cubic-inch flathead straight eight with 150 horsepower, or a 327-cid with 165 hp.

Below: High-mount taillights identified '54 Clippers like this Super Panama hardtop.

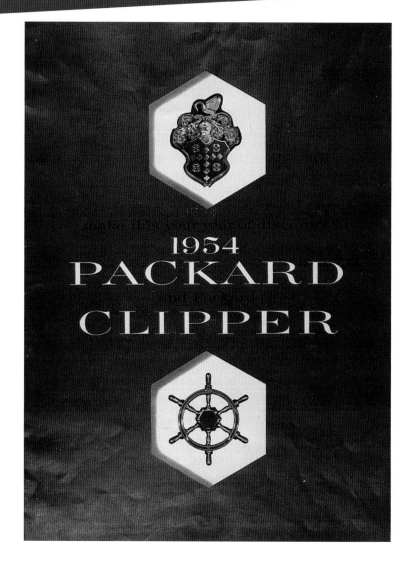

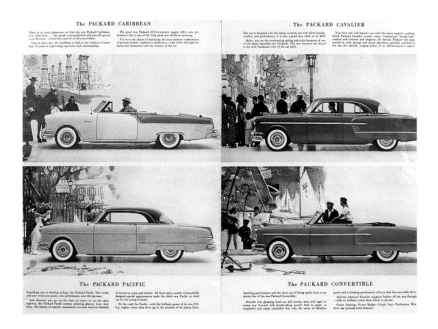

Packard's big cars rode a 127-inch wheelbase (vs. Clipper's 122), but three models carried "big car" styling on the shorter wheelbase: the standard convertible; a high-price, low-volume "deluxe" version of the convertible called the Caribbean; and the Pacific hardtop coupe. All three were powered by a new 359-cid straight eight with 212 hp, as was the topline $3890 Patrician sedan. Also depicted in this brochure is the $3344 Cavalier, the Patrician's less expensive sibling, which carried a 327-cid straight eight with 185 hp.

The Caribbean had been introduced in 1953 as a $5210 specialty convertible to rival similar cars from General Motors, and it continued for '54 with a staggering $6100 price tag. Only 400 were sold.

Above: Like the costly Caribbean, Packard's $3827 Pacific hardtop had the big 359-cid engine. This one has dealer-installed air conditioning. During the year, Ultra-matic was modified for low-gear start, and tubeless tires became standard.

Left: Depicted on this 1954 brochure is Studebaker's beautiful Starliner hardtop coupe. Offered in both the Champion and top-line Commander series, they were priced at $2241 and $2502, respectively. All Champions were powered by a frugal 169-cubic-inch 85-horsepower flathead six, while Commanders got a 232-cid 127-hp overhead-valve V-8.

Right: Arriving for 1954 was Studebaker's first station wagon, the two-door Conestoga. It was available in both the Champion and Commander lines with prices ranging from $2187 to $2556. Both lines also offered two- and four-door sedans priced from $1758 to $2438.

Below: For $161 less than corresponding Starliner hard-top coupes, buyers could get a pillared Starlight coupe in either Champion or Commander trim.

1955

Few years rival 1955 as a boom season, or for signaling cultural shifts that were quickly taking place—in and out of the auto industry.

Close to seven out of the 10 families had an automobile (or even two). The horsepower race was in full swing, led by the new Chrysler 300—so named for its engine output. Kaiser-Willys Corporation was now the only automaker without a V-8 engine.

Legislation was introduced to make seatbelts required. Ford and Chrysler announced dealer-installed belts. Dealers in 311 cities launched a free safety program, aiming at two million vehicles. The American Automobile Association halted sanctioning of auto races, and urged manufacturers to emphasize safety, not speed. Michigan was the first state to require a driver's education course before issuing a license to youths under 18.

Even though today's enthusiasts can easily discern a Ford from a Chevrolet, a Buick from a DeSoto, experts at the time expressed dismay about the growing similarities among car models. The wrapped windshield, for one, suggested to some critics that automakers were merely following each other's lead—imitating rather than innovating.

In fact, each make had fewer unique mechanical features than in past seasons. Therefore, ads pushed styling, size, price, and power, along with less-tangible inducements such as status and comfort. Dealers began to decry the profusion of color and option possibilities, complaining that they couldn't stock enough cars to satisfy starry-eyed customers—who found it harder than ever to make up their minds.

Wages had been rising faster than car prices ever since the end of World War II. The average full-time worker now earned $76 a week, or $3851 per year. More than half of families took in over $5000 yearly, up from one-third of families in 1950. Unemployment was no cause for concern, dipping below four percent.

The first McDonald's was erected in 1955—though few dared predict its eventual impact on American culture. Colonel Sanders had Kentucky Fried Chicken restaurants under way, and Disneyland opened in Anaheim, California. Kids wore Davy Crockett hats, in response to a TV series about the frontier hero. Male teens turned to pink shirts and charcoal gray suits with "pegged" (narrow) cuffs.

Marty won the Oscar for best picture—and its star, Ernest Borgnine, took best-actor honors. James Dean starred in three films before his untimely death in an automobile accident on September 30. Meanwhile, Elizabeth Taylor married singer Eddie Fisher.

Fats Domino warbled "Ain't That a Shame," the Platters crooned "Only You," and Chuck Berry rocked his ode to "Maybelline." TV premieres included *The Honeymooners* with Jackie Gleason, and Bob Keeshin's *Captain Kangaroo*. Annette Funicello led *The Mickey Mouse Club*, and *Gunsmoke* debuted as the first "adult" western. A few critics condemned the jungle of TV antennas dotting rooftops, but most Americans eagerly sampled the latest video wares.

Housewives, not yet taking to the workforce in droves, were encouraged to own all the latest labor-saving gadgets, so families might have more leisure time— perhaps to tour the countryside in that dazzling new piece of Detroit iron. In fact, the Ethyl Corporation launched a "Drive More" campaign to encourage consumption of gasoline.

Auto dealers pushed hard to secure those record-breaking sales in '55, sometimes cutting their markups to the bone in a quest for volume. More than 61 million vehicles were on the road, eight million of them more than 15 years old. One-fourth of the American fleet had seen more than seven seasons, and were thus prime candidates for replacement with a spanking-new hardtop or sedan.

Detroit had another round of restylings in the wings to grab a few million more sales. But danger for dealers—and the industry—lay ahead. Not only did the Senate begin to probe merchandising techniques, led by subcommittee chairman Mike Monroney, but investigators alleged that GM might qualify as a monopoly—subject to forced breakup.

American Motors Corporation

Hudson originally planned to introduce a mere update to the Step-down design for 1955, but the merger with Nash brought an entirely different car.

And this was it. Bodyshells were shared with Nash, but aside from the reverse-slant rear roof pillar, it was hard to tell; both makes sported wildly different front and rear styling. Hudson arguably got the better end of the deal, yet its sales went down while Nash's went up. Shown is a top-line Hornet in two-door-hardtop guise; there was no more convertible. With the standard 2 308-cubic-inch flathead six with 160/170 horsepower or the newly available 320-cid V-8 with 208, Hornet prices ranged from $2565 to $3145.

Wasps again looked similar, but rode a shorter wheelbase and came with a not-very-sporty 202-cid six with 110-120 hp. Shown is the $2460 Custom sedan. All Hudsons adopted Nash's famous Weather-Eye heating and ventilation system.

Beautiful performers—new Hudson Hornet Hollywood hardtop (available with V-8 or Championship Six engine) and Star Water-Ski Performers of Cypress Gardens, Winter Haven, Florida.

Beautiful, new Hudsons by American Motors give you all these extras . . . at no extra cost!

Extra room, ride, vision, and safety . . . top big list of features found nowhere else at any price!

HUDSON   OTHER MAKES

Hudson seats are wider than those in any other car at any price—nearly six inches of extra room in many cases! Headroom is again the best in any car at any price—three inches more than in some of the most expensive cars built today! See it for yourself.

Extra-smooth, steady ride. Hudson brings you American Motors' exclusive, new Deep Coil Ride—at no extra cost. Long-coil springs, with three times ordinary cushioning power, slanted outward for new anti-sway safety—for smoother riding, easier handling.

Widest wrap-around windshield—you get extra vision-area in Hudson—easier, more relaxed driving. The widest wrap-around windshield in the business (completely free from distortion anywhere) teams up with a new lowered hood to give you perfect forward vision. Hudson fenders are raised to help guide you in tight spots and in parking.

HUDSON   OTHER MAKES

Extra safety, longer car life with American Motors' exclusive Double Strength Single Unit car construction—rattleproof, twice as strong, twice as rigid, twice as safe as other bolted-together bodies and frames. Keeps Hudson like new longer—makes it a better trade-in.

Hudson Hornet · Wasp · Rambler · Metropolitan
Products of American Motors

See "Disneyland," great new all-family show, ABC-TV network. Check TV listings for time and station.

Left: Hudson ads boasted that its full-sized offerings had the widest seats and most head room of any car—odd, since Nash's Ambassador had the same body.

Below: Hudson dealers must have rejoiced when they got their first batch of popular Ramblers, despite the fact they differed from Nashes mainly in grille badging. It's doubtful competing Nash dealers were quite as enthused. Ramblers had an economy-minded 195-cubic-inch six with 90 horsepower and were priced as low as $1457, though Custom models like those shown cost close to two grand.

A Hudson Statesman enters as a Hudson Rambler (a name that surely raised the ire of Nash dealers) leaves.

Below: Nash's dashboard retained its center-focused styling theme, with the speedometer offset to the right of the steering wheel. This Statesman is equipped with air conditioning, an option to Nash's excellent Weather-Eye heating and ventilation system.

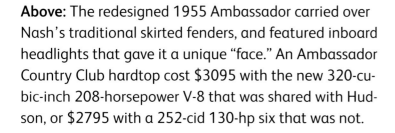

Above: The redesigned 1955 Ambassador carried over Nash's traditional skirted fenders, and featured inboard headlights that gave it a unique "face." An Ambassador Country Club hardtop cost $3095 with the new 320-cubic-inch 208-horsepower V-8 that was shared with Hudson, or $2795 with a 252-cid 130-hp six that was not.

As before, the Statesman mirrored Ambassador styling, but on a shorter wheelbase.

Above: Rambler's value equation was a strong selling point. Not only was the car inexpensive to buy and run, but resale value had been high as well. Prices started at $1585—about the same as a really stripped '55 Chevrolet—with air conditioning and automatic transmission optional.

Right: Top-line Rambler sedans and coupes shared their big brother's reverse-slant rear roof pillar. Lower-level models had a traditional sloping roof pillar. Nash's Rambler outsold Hudson's version by more than nine-to-one, and outsold all other Nashes combined.

A Custom Cross Country wagon was the most expensive Rambler at $2098.

Chrysler Corporation

Right: Virgil Exner took over Chrysler Corporation's styling department in the late Forties, and the redesigned '55 models were the first to show off his radical Forward Look. And radical it was, particularly when compared to the rather dowdy appearance for which the corporation had become known. Topping the Chrysler line was the performance-oriented 300, named for its horsepower output—the highest of any Detroit make that year. As such, it led the blossoming "horsepower race," and made Chryslers the dominant force in stock-car racing. At $4110, however, it was a pricey machine for well-heeled performance connoisseurs, and only 1725 were sold. The 300 shared its large, split grille with the Imperial, which was spun off as a separate make for 1955.

Below: A New Yorker Deluxe Newport two-door coupe (shown) shared the 300's body, but carried the standard Chrysler grille and a 250-hp version of the 331-cubic-inch Hemi V-8. It also carried a $3652 sticker price. Windsor Deluxe remained the entry-level series, but its traditional six-cylinder engine was replaced by a 301-cid polyspherical-head V-8 rated at 225/250 hp that was less efficient—and cheaper to build—than the Hemi.

Chrome fins topped tall taillights as Chrysler followed an industry trend. The New Yorker St. Regis two-door hardtop wore different side trim and paint scheme than the Newport, and cost $38 more.

DeSoto arguably fared even better than Chrysler with its new Exner styling. Fireflite became the new top-rung model, with Firedome relegated to entry-level status. Both were powered by a 291-cubic-inch Hemi V-8 with 185 or 200 horsepower. This Fireflite Sportsman hardtop coupe listed for $2939.

A station wagon was available only in the Firedome series. DeSoto and Dodge offered the industry's first three-tone paint treatments, this wagon's third color being the gray band surrounding the windows.

The "spring special" Fireflite Coronado came only as a four-door sedan with its own black, white, and turquoise tri-tone paint scheme.

DeSotos featured a pleasing dual-pod dash with round gauges set ahead of the driver.

By contrast, Dodge's design spread the gauges across the dash.

Dodge ads for '55 extolled the virtues of the car's New Horizon sweep-around windshield, and promised that its virtues could be yours "for little more than many models of the 'low priced three'"—taking an indirect stab at its own Plymouth stablemate.

Above: Imperial became a separate make for 1955, but shared its large eggcrate grille with the Chrysler 300. Unique, however, were its "gun sight" taillights perched atop the rear fenders. Power came from the same 331-cid 250-hp Hemi V-8 found in Chryslers. A stately four-door sedan cost $4483.

Below: The long-wheelbase (149.5 inches) Crown Imperial was sold mainly as a limousine, as its $7000 sticker precluded many personal-car sales.

Dodge's new top-of-the-line series was the Custom Royal, followed by the Royal and Coronet. Only the Coronet was available with the 230-cubic-inch six, now making 123 horsepower. All others came with a 270-cid V-8, though there were two versions: Custom Royals got a Hemi with 183/193 hp, others a non-hemi-head version with 175. A Custom Royal convertible cost $2748; a two-door hardtop was a couple hundred dollars less.

With no convertible in the line, the most expensive "regular" Imperial was the $4720 Newport hardtop coupe.

all-new

'55 PLYMOUTH

the biggest car in Plymouth history...longer, lower, wider!

Of all Chrysler Corp. makes, Plymouth underwent the greatest transformation for '55. Not only did it boast a striking, modern look, but it also received its first V-8. Called Hy-Fire, the wedgehead engine (it wasn't a Hemi) arrived in two displacements: 241 and 260 cubic inches, with ratings from 157 to 177 horsepower.

The symmetrical dashboard got round gauges, and when the optional automatic transmission was ordered, it also got a dash-mounted shift lever, referred to in ads as the "PowerFlite Range Selector."

Oddly, '55 Plymouths kept the same model names as their dowdy predecessors. Belvedere again topped the lineup, this sport coupe starting at $2217. Three-tone paint schemes weren't offered, but two-tones—in a rather odd pattern—were.

Above: While the cheapest six-cylinder Plaza sedan started at $1781, this top-line Belvedere sedan sold slightly better—at $200 more.

Below: Another Belvedere sedan was chosen as a test mule for an experimental turbine-engine conversion. It never made production, but it became the first turbine-powered car to be driven on American streets.

Ford Motor Company

Nineteen fifty-five was a big year for Ford. A complete restyle brought subtle tailfins and a fresh look—plus some unusual two-tone paint schemes. The $2224 Sunliner convertible was now part of the new top-line Fairlane series, which replaced the Crestline.

Left: Also exclusive to the Fairlane series was the $2202 Crown Victoria hardtop, which featured a brushed-metal roof band. The front half of the roof could be converted to tinted glass for an extra $70.

Below: The least expensive Fairlane was the $1914 two-door Club Sedan. Mainline and Customline models could be ordered with an enlarged 272-cubic-inch V-8 with 162 to 182 horsepower, but Fairlanes could be optioned with a 292-cid version with 198 horses. That was nearly double the maximum horsepower offered in a Ford as recently as 1951.

Above: What was called the Country Sedan wasn't a sedan at all, but a wagon with six- or eight-passenger seating. They retailed for $2156 and $2287, respectively. All wagons were now grouped in their own series, which also included the two-door Ranch and four-door Country Squire.

Right: The all-new 1955 Thunderbird carried design cues taken from the rest of the Ford line. The fender louvers were just decoration, but the hood scoop was functional. Note the spinner-style bumper guards, mesh grille, browed headlights, and rally-flag hood emblem. Wire wheel covers were a factory option.

Perhaps Ford's biggest news for 1955 was the introduction of the Thunderbird. The two-seater was intended to go head-to-head with Chevrolet's Corvette, but it was hardly a fair fight: The amply equipped T-Bird outsold the rudimentary—and similarly priced—'Vette by a whopping 23:1 margin. A 292-cubic-inch V-8 good for 193 horsepower (198 with automatic transmission) was standard in the T-Bird.

Ford Motor Company chairman Henry Ford II steps out of a '55 T-Bird.

Right: Dashboards were simple and functional. Note the tachometer.

Below: Lincoln underwent a radical makeover for 1955 that made it look longer and sleeker despite an unchanged wheelbase. Much of that was due to extended tailfins capping tall, "cathedral" taillights, coincidentally similar to those adopted by Packard. A top-line Capri convertible—Lincoln's priciest car—cost $4072.

Though it was a two-seat convertible, Ford shied away from calling the Thunderbird a "sports car," instead preferring to call it a "personal car." Available T-Bird amenities included a telescopic steering column, power seat, and lift-off hardtop.

A personal car of distinction . . .
FORD THUNDERBIRD

"Frenched" headlights encircled in chrome and a simple, horizontal-bar grille gave Lincoln's front end a classier look. So did a stately chrome-and-gold hood ornament.

Speaking of the hood, it covered a 341-cubic-inch V-8 rated at 225 horsepower, up from '54's 317 with 205 hp. This 1955 Capri two-door hardtop listed for $3910.

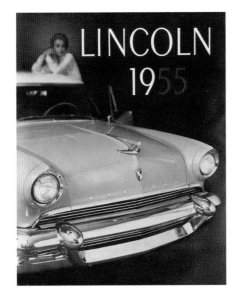

It was easy to recognize the restyled 1955 Mercury thanks to its hooded headlights and revised grille. Monterey was relegated to midline status as Montclair became the top dog. This glass-topped Montclair Sun Valley sold for $2712, about $450 more than its Ford counterpart.

Right: The squared-off rear fenders and taller taillights fitted to '55 Mercs are shown on an entry-level $2218 Custom two-door sedan.

Below: Those who missed the woody wagons of the early '50s could get their $2844 Monterey wagon fitted with woodgrain trim.

MERCURY'S NEW MONTCLAIR SERIES

Mercury's top four-door sedan was the $2685 Montclair.

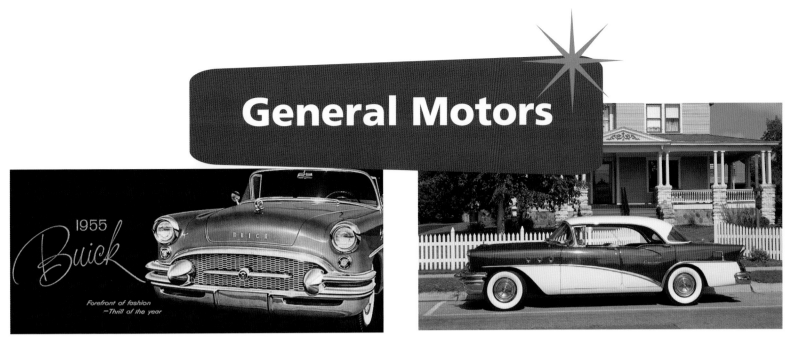

General Motors

Buicks were redesigned for 1955, and wore their revised lines particularly well. Front ends took on a Cadillac character with a massive chrome grille and bumper accented with bullet-shaped bumper extensions. Augmenting the returning two- and four-door sedans, two-door hardtops and convertibles, and four-door wagons was a new four-door hardtop without center roof pillars. Referred to as the Riviera hardtop sedan, it's shown here in entry-level Special trim, attractively priced at $2409 with a 188-horsepower 264-cubic-inch V-8.

Above: Centurys continued as the hot-rod Buick, hosting the larger 322-cid V-8 found in top-line Roadmasters in the shorter, lighter Special body. Horsepower of this engine was raised to 236 for 1955, making Century a potent pursuit vehicle.

Below: A "hauler" in every sense of the word was this $3175 Century station wagon.

While "everyday" Cadillacs continued into 1955 with few changes, the exotic Eldorado received a unique tail treatment that foreshadowed what its stablemates would get three years hence. At $6286, the Eldo remained staggeringly expensive.

Above: Eldorados featured an exclusive rear-end treatment with prominent "shark" fins and Sabre-Spoke wheels instead of wires. Under the hood sat a 270-bhp version of the V-8 breathing through twin four-barrel carbs. "Limited" production totaled 3950 cars.

Below: The Series 62 four-door sedan retained its title as the most popular Cadillac, but wouldn't for much longer. All Caddys got a horsepower boost for 1955, setting the standard cars at 250, the Eldorado at 270.

Those who blanched at the Eldorado's price could save nearly $1800 by picking a Series 62 convertible.

Chevy's 1955 brochure exclaimed "New Everything!"— and it wasn't an exaggeration. Besides the all-new look, the company released its first V-8 in 35 years: a short-stroke, overhead-valve wonder that would carry on in its basic form for more than four decades. Sized at 265 cubic inches, it produced as much as 180 horsepower. Still offered as the base engine was a 235-cid six.

On November 23, 1954, a special gold-trimmed '55 Bel Air became the 50-millionth General Motors car to roll off an assembly line.

Newly offered by Chevrolet was the two-door Nomad wagon, which would become among the most collectible of the '55 closed models. It was available only as a top-line Bel Air at $2472.

A $2206 Bel Air convertible is shown decked out with optional continental kit, which moved the spare tire to an enclosed case mounted on the rear bumper. A similar car paced the 1955 running of the Indy 500.

Corvette got a much-needed injection of power in the form of Chevy's new V-8, which offered 195 hp. Also available (finally) was a three-speed manual transmission. Yet sales sank to just 674—mostly due to Ford's new Thunderbird.

After being updated for 1954, Oldsmobile entered 1955 with relatively minor changes. This put it at a disadvantage against the rash of redesigned vehicles introduced that year, especially since it didn't get much help in the powertrain department: The top 324-cubic-inch Rocket V-8 gained a modest (for 1955) 18 horsepower, coming in at 202. Yet amazingly, Olds not only held its own, but advanced—from fifth place to fourth in industry sales. The Ninety-Eight Starfire convertible remained the most expensive Olds at $3276.

At the opposite end of the hardtop price spectrum was the 88 Holiday hardtop coupe at $2474.

Above: Newly available for 1955 was a four-door hardtop, what Olds called a Holiday hardtop sedan. It was offered in all series—88, Super 88, and Ninety-Eight—and cost $186 to $307 more than a comparable four-door pillared sedan. That was quite a lot in 1955 dollars, yet the four-door hardtops sold very well. This Ninety-Eight Holiday hardtop sedan went for $3140.

Below: A plain-Jane 88 two-door sedan—devoid of two-tone lower-body paint or whitewall tires—is a rare sight today. In 1955, it was Oldsmobile's entry-level model at $2297.

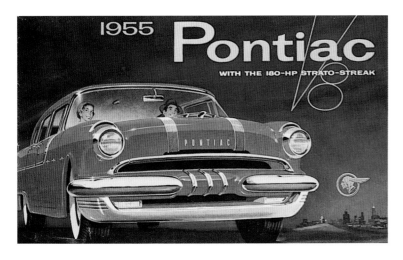

Pontiacs took on a whole new look for 1955 yet retained many signature styling cues. Sleek side panels culminated in a kick-up at the rear, beneath which sat the traditional round taillights. Hoods wore the usual "silver streaks," though they now ran in two rows. Also new was the company's first V-8. The 287-cubic-inch overhead-valve Strato-Streak made 180 horsepower, or 200 with optional four-barrel carburetor. A Starchief Custom Catalina hardtop coupe listed at $2499.

Above: Although rooflines were shared with Chevy, Pontiac had its own character, as a glance at this 1955 Star Chief two-door hardtop makes clear. The optional hood ornament now had a larger amber segment, and three body-side stars signaled it was a Star Chief.

Below: The ability to drop the top on your Star Chief cost an extra $192.

Newly installed as Pontiac's most expensive car was the $2962 Custom Safari wagon. It mimicked Chevy's Nomad wagon in having two doors and semi-hardtop styling, but rode a longer wheelbase and cost $500 more.

Kaiser-Willys Corporation

A lone Manhattan carried the Kaiser banner into 1955, but a mild "taillift" wasn't enough to save it, and Kaiser bowed out.

Willys got a revised grille for 1955, when four-cylinder versions were dropped. Added as a topline model was the Bermuda, shown here in two-door hardtop form. These sporty-looking models sold for $1895 to $1997, far too much to be popular. The Willys Aero died in the United States along with Kaiser, but other Willys products under the Jeep name would transfer to other owners, and of course, the name continues to this day.

Kaiser-Willys billed its newly renamed Willys Bermuda as the cheapest American-built hardtop, starting as low as $1895—far less than the previous Eagle hardtop. Only 2215 were produced, most of them carrying Kaiser's 115-horsepower Super Hurricane engine. Showy two-tone paint was available, too. No self-respecting manufacturer could think of surviving long without dazzling color choices on tap—but nothing could help Willys hang on any longer.

Studebaker-Packard Corporation

With Packard's 1955 styling changes and new V-8 engine came renewed interest in its senior cars, which now included the Patrician sedan (shown in ad), Four Hundred hardtop coupe, and Caribbean convertible, all on a 127-inch wheelbase. This ad promotes Packard's new Torsion-Level suspension, which consisted of longitudinal torsion bars that replaced conventional coil springs and included a system for automatic leveling regardless of load.

Above: A deft facelift of the 1951-54 bodyshell resulted in what looked like an all-new Packard for 1955. Clippers kept their tail treatment but adopted a slightly altered version of the senior Packard's restyled front end. Also new were Torsion-Level ride, and—at last—a modern overhead-valve V-8. Two sizes went into Clippers: 320 cubic inches with 225 horsepower, or 352 cid with 245 hp.

Below: Topping the Clipper line was the $3076 Constellation hardtop coupe. Other Clippers could be had for as little as $2586.

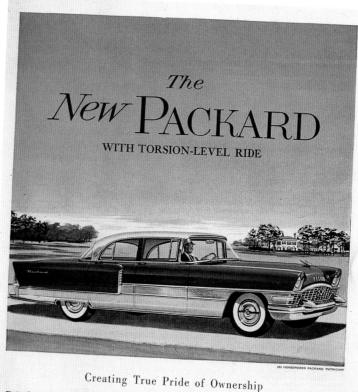

Packard's specialty convertible, the pricey Caribbean, was actually a little less pricey for 1955. It was rolled back from $6100 to $5932, despite having moved to the longer wheelbase.

Completing the senior Packard line was the $3930 Four Hundred hardtop coupe.

In a year when most every car sported a radical new look, Studebaker entered 1955 with warmed-over models...and sales inexplicably skyrocketed. The former long-wheelbase Land Cruiser sedan gave way to a line of two- and four-door models under the President name. Tops among them was the $3253 Speedster hardtop coupe, which was fitted with a new 259-cubic-inch V-8 making 185 horsepower; in other Presidents, it made 175 hp. Speedsters came with flamboyant two-tone paint, quilted leather upholstery, and an "engine-turned" instrument panel.

Originally a show model, the rakish President Speedster saw limited production for '55. Note the exclusive "tri-level" paint and wide chrome band over the rear portion of the roof.

A 1955 ad points out that Studebakers were available with all kinds of power—for windows, brakes, steering, and seat. It also shows off the bulky chrome snout fitted to all Studebakers that year.

Champions, including this Conestoga wagon, had a larger 185-cubic-inch six with 101 horsepower. Commanders started 1955 with a smaller 224-cid V-8 with 140 hp, but later in the model year got the President's 259 detuned to 162 hp.

Champion four-door sedans were priced from $1783 to $1993—right in line with comparable Chevrolets.

1956

Executive suites were full of gray flannel suits as avid strivers began their ascensions up corporate ladders—seen as the only way to travel. Even in factories and clerical offices, though, the overall mood remained unabashedly optimistic.

Sure, an occasional critic unearthed a flaw or two in the national character. William Whyte, for one, questioned the drive toward corporate conformity in his book, *The Organization Man*. Still, despite an occasional setback, prosperity was obviously here to stay—wasn't it?

Lincoln led the way with a major revamp for its regular line—plus the rebirth of the Continental, a name unused since 1948. Thus, Lincoln mounted a strong challenge to Cadillac's well-deserved reputation for reliability and high resale value.

Rambler, too, was all-new, as it dropped its two-door models to concentrate on four-doors—including the industry's first hardtop station wagon. Otherwise, with the exception of Studebaker's Hawk series, other makes sported only the traditional facelift. But there was more than just fresh styling to tempt new-car buyers.

Horsepower was big news, topped by Chrysler's second-edition supercar: the 300-B. DeSoto, Dodge, and Plymouth issued semi-supercars, and nearly every make advertised major power boosts. Many engines grew in displacement, but Packard's V-8 beat them all, reaching a then-whopping 374 cubic inches.

Comfort played an ever-larger role, and a dozen makes offered leather interiors. Transistor radios began to elbow aside the old vacuum-tube units. Ed Cole, soon to be named Chevrolet's general manager, predicted a trend toward fuel injection and lighter engines.

The 156-mile Indiana Toll Road opened, joining the Ohio Turnpike to create a Chicago-New York superhighway. Meanwhile, a 41,000-mile interstate highway system was approved, with the federal government prepared to pay 90 percent of the cost. A five-man team of legislators visited Detroit, hinting at the prospect of a safe-car law.

Industry output eased to 6.3 million cars. Even so, America now had as many registered cars as households—a figure predicted to rise steadily as the notion of a "second car" grabbed hold.

Imports continued their gradual influence on the market. Volvo sent its PV544 from Sweden, Germany marketed a little Lloyd, unorthodox Citroëns began to arrive from France—and Volkswagen sales grew steadily.

Car prices rose this year—some substantially. So despite continued wage increases, not everyone could come up with the cash—or secure sufficient credit—to drive home a spanking-new '56. Going secondhand was the only answer. Once considered a "problem" by franchised dealers, used cars were now a vital element of the auto trade, and a blessing to lower-income families in need of "cheap wheels."

On a lighter note, ads for Clairol hair coloring wondered: "Does she or doesn't she?" TV viewers could now see *As the World Turns* and *The Price is Right*. They also took a liking to such quiz shows as *The $64,000 Challenge* and *$64,000 Question*, which would blossom into scandal a few years later.

Out Hollywood way, Carroll Baker's sensual performance in *Baby Doll*—which would barely warrant a raised eyebrow today—startled '56 moviegoers. No less shocking was the steamy best-selling novel, *Peyton Place*.

Public tastes generally leaned toward far tamer fare, such as best-picture Oscar winner *Around the World in 80 Days*. Future president John F. Kennedy won a Pulitzer Prize for his collection of biographical essays, *Profiles in Courage*.

James Dean was gone, but his last movie, the epic *Giant*, earned a best-director award. Meanwhile, the eyes of the world focused on former actress Grace Kelly, as she exchanged storybook marital vows with Monaco's Prince Rainier. Playwright Arthur Miller took Marilyn Monroe as his lawful wife.

Mothers could now buy disposable diapers, owners of noisy cars could hit a Midas Muffler shop, and airlines carried as many passengers as railroads. Private cars remained king, and Detroit's designers were busy with some special treats for '57.

American Motors Corporation

IT'S HERE!..THE BIG CAR WITH BIG CHANGES

THE NEW 1956 HUDSON HORNET WITH THE NEW V-8

Alive with new V-8 power! Sleek with new V-Line styling! Luxurious with new, high-fashion, color-matched exteriors and interiors!

HUDSON HORNET V-8

The most beautiful performer of them all!

Hudson was trying really hard—perhaps too hard—to keep up with the flashy new offerings from the Big Three. The 1956 Hornet added small fins to its front and rear fenders, could be ordered in 15 two-tone and six three-tone color combinations, and adopted a huge "smiling" grille. But it turned out there would be little to smile about, as for all this effort, sales of the big Hudsons (Hornet and Wasp) retreated to less than 11,000 units—about half the '55 total. Hornet's available V-8 first grew to 352 cubic inches and 220 horsepower, then was replaced by a 250-cid, 190-hp engine.

Designed in-house, Hudson's instrument cluster looked relatively plain for this gaudy period—especially when compared to the garish body.

A Continental-style outside spare remained available on full-size models. Styled by consultant Richard Arbib, the '56 Hudsons were viewed by many as excessive—or even bizarre, bordering on grotesque.

Hudson and Nash continued as the only makes to offer reclining seats that converted into twin beds—popular with drive-in movie patrons and outdoor types.

Hardtops never were a high-volume item at Hudson, so only 1640 Hornet Hollywoods were built this season. The huge eggcrate grille was interrupted by a "V" carrying the Hudson emblem at the top, dipping in another V-shape at the bottom. A small chrome fin topped each taillight.

A redesigned Rambler boasted considerably altered styling, but it's hard to say it was an improvement. Whether wearing a Nash or Hudson badge, sales didn't come close to matching 1955's figures. Body styles were trimmed to include only four-doors: a sedan, a wagon, a hardtop sedan, and the nation's first hardtop wagon. Prices went up, now starting at $1829, but the sales decline may have been due more to its association with the names Hudson and Nash, which were sinking fast.

The Nash Rambler was very much like the Hudson Rambler—except it sold better. Though the wheelbase remained at 108 inches, same as the longer of the two '55 versions, the new Rambler looked bigger—a questionable strategy for what had made its name as a compact car. New to the line were a four-door hardtop and a four-door hardtop wagon. Though the six-cylinder engine remained at 195 cubic inches, a switch from a flathead configuration to overhead valves boosted horsepower from 90 to 120. The least expensive sedan went for $1829, just $40 less than a comparable '56 Chevrolet. Sales score: Rambler, 10,000. Chevy, 1.5 million. Hmm.

Only 2155 Rambler Custom hardtop sedans were produced. Note the duo-color roof band.

For $1939, Rambler's mid-range Super sedan had less brightwork and a plainer interior than the Custom.

Ads promised much that was new and different in a Rambler, from the Fashion Safety Arch to the Typhoon engine and enhanced visibility. Power steering was now optional.

Nash needed a stylish new design to bounce back from a rather dismal 1955. It didn't get it. But with sales so poor, it's surprising the company spent the money to do anything at all. Rear ends were taller and more squared off, front ends added vertical parking light pods at the forward edge of the fenders.

Midyear brought an Ambassador Special series, including this $2462 Country Club hardtop.

Above: A four-door sedan was the only body style in the Ambassador Super Six series, priced at $2425.

Below: Late in the '56 model year, the tiny Metropolitan imported from England was updated with a slightly revised front end and a larger 90-cubic-inch, 52-horsepower engine.

Once in their lives everyone should drive a '50s car, so that on a handling scale of 1 to 10, they'll know what a zero feels like. A '56 Nash will do nicely.

Chrysler Corporation

18 GLEAMING FEET OF POWER...
EAGER TO CALL YOU MASTER

THE WINDSOR NEWPORT IN STARDUST BLUE AND CLOUD WHITE

THE NEW "PowerStyle" CHRYSLER FOR 1956

You can actually see the thrilling power in this breathtaking new Chrysler.

See it in every fresh, sleek "PowerStyle" line.

See it in the dynamic, pulse-quickening look that says clearly and unmistakably, "Here is the world's greatest performing car!"

And how brilliantly just a few moments behind the wheel bear out that promise. Instantly, you discover a brand-new sense of driving mastery. A new and exciting

feeling of complete control never before possible in any car. You're *the boss!*

For here you command the surging power of Chrysler's exclusive airplane-type V-8 engine with the ultra-efficient hemispherical combustion chamber . . . plus new Push-button PowerFlite automatic transmission which you control simply by pushing a button on the dash! You get a full-time power-assist from Chrysler's new Power-Pilot Steering — a constant, positive, pre-

dictable feel-of-the-road. And you get the safest, most velvety braking with still another "Forward Look" advance — new Power-Smooth Brakes that last twice as long as any others.

We invite you now to enjoy this never-to-be-forgotten experience in driving mastery, and we promise you a new sense of conquest over space. Take your first ride in the magnificent new "PowerStyle" Chrysler. See your Chrysler dealer today!

NOW MORE THAN EVER . . . AMERICA'S MOST SMARTLY DIFFERENT CAR

Above: New Yorker's Hemi V-8 was enlarged to 354 cubic inches, bringing 280 horses along for the ride. Chrysler joined DeSoto and Dodge in offering three-tone paint combinations, as shown on this $3931 New Yorker Newport hardtop coupe.

Left: "Power Style" Chryslers wore taller tailfins for 1956, courtesy of a facelift that actually improved upon the '55 redesign.

Windsor—like New Yorker, now minus the "Deluxe" surname—was again the entry-level Chrysler, and the $2870 Windsor sedan was again the top-selling model. Joining the four-door sedan was a new four-door hardtop (in both Windsor and New Yorker trim), which did away with the sedan's center roof pillar. Windsors also got a displacement increase for '56, now with a 331-cid V-8 making 225 or 250 hp.

Chrysler's mighty 300 returned for 1956 with even more muscle. Newly named the 300-B, its 354 Hemi was tuned for 340 horsepower in standard form, 355 with optional dual four-barrel carburetors—making it the first American car to boast one horsepower per cubic inch, a long-standing target for efficiency. Still, the $4419 300-B was an expensive specialty car that garnered a mere 1102 orders.

An unusual Chrysler option was Highway Hi Fi, a record player mounted beneath the center of the dashboard. It played special seven-inch records at 16 ⅔ rpm.

All '56 Chrysler Corp. cars with automatic transmission traded their dash-mounted shift levers for now-famous pushbuttons mounted in a pod on the left side of the dashboard. There was no Park button, so the parking brake got a workout.

DeSoto got its own "halo car" for 1956 in the form of the gold-trimmed Adventurer. DeSoto's standard V-8 grew to 330 cubic inches and 230/255 horsepower for '56, but the Adventurer got a 341-cid version good for 320 hp. Adventurer copied the flavor of Chrysler's 300-B, but at a significantly lower price—$3728 vs. $4419.

At mid-season, DeSoto issued just under a thousand lavish, high-performance Adventurer hardtops, sporting gold-anodized trim.

A new body style introduced in all Chrysler Corp. makes for '56 was the four-door hardtop sedan. Lacking a middle roof pillar gave it the sportier look of a two-door hardtop while maintaining the easier rear-seat access of a four-door. This stunning Fireflite Sportsman hardtop sedan started at $3431. It's equipped with optional air conditioning—which was mounted in the trunk—as evidenced by the small scoop beside the rear roof pillar and the cold-air outlet behind the rear seat. On a historical note, it was a Fireflite convertible that paced the Indy 500 in 1956—the only time a DeSoto was so honored.

Above: Dodge flexed its muscles for '56 with the potent D-500 option. It brought the newly enlarged 315-cubic-inch Super Red Ram V-8, but fitted it with a four-barrel carburetor for 230 horsepower—or 260 with high-compression heads.

Below: D-500 was optional on all models, and turned the lightweight Dodge into a fearsome street performer.

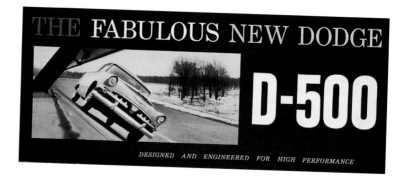

In what was becoming an annual event, Dodge's "spring special" for '56 was the Golden Lancer, a trim package for the top-line Custom Royal Lancer hardtop coupe. A crossed-flag "500" insignia on the trunk identified the D-500 option.

"The Magic Touch of Tomorrow" was Dodge's announcement of new pushbutton activation for its automatic transmission. Not mentioned in the ad was Dodge's equally new four-door hardtop sedan.

The lowest-priced Dodge was a Coronet two-door sedan, which started at $2194 in six-cylinder form. It was also available with a 270-cid 189-hp V-8 for $103 more.

Wagons were offered as the two-door Suburban or four-door Sierra. For cost reasons, '56 wagons retained the '55 rear-end treatment.

Above: Imperial kept its "gun sight" taillights for '56, which now sat atop taller fins. Underhood was Chrysler's 354 Hemi with 280 hp, but backing it was a new three-speed automatic, the first of the legendary TorqueFlites.

Below: Two- and four-door wagons were grouped under the Suburban model name for '56. This line-topping $2484 Suburban Sport shows off that year's new taillight treatment.

Like its corporate brothers, Plymouths wore taller tailfins for '56. Also like its stablemates, the available V-8 engines grew in size and power. The former 241- and 260-cubic-inch V-8s were replaced by 270- and 277-cid units with 180-200 horsepower. Still standard on most models was a 230-cid six, now with 125 hp. A top-line Belvedere convertible listed for $2478.

A midyear arrival was the aptly named Fury. Offered only in white with gold anodized trim, the Fury was fitted with a 240-hp 303-cid V-8 that powered it to a couple of stock-car records—certainly not the kind of achievement usually associated with stodgy old Plymouth. It made such an impact that the Fury name continued to grace Plymouth models through the end of the 1980s.

Ford Motor Company

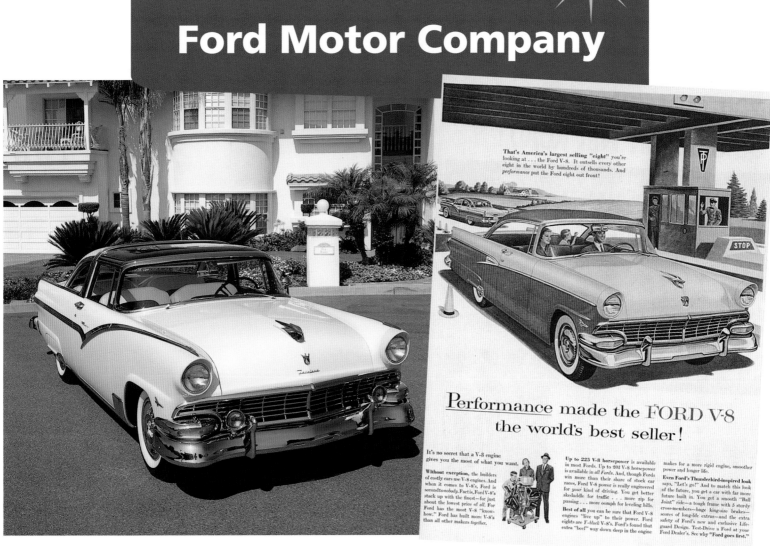

Performance made the FORD V-8 the world's best seller!

Like most makes that were redesigned for 1955, Fords received only a mild facelift for '56. Sales of the glass-topped Fairlane Crown Victoria were down by two-thirds to a mere 603, perhaps due to their reputation for being mobile ovens.

Above: Ford heavily promoted its Y-Block V-8 (introduced for '54), though many of its cars were sold with the standard 223-cubic-inch six. For 1956, a 312-cid version of the V-8 was added to the carryover 272 and 292, with horse-power outputs now ranging from 173 to 215. Shown front and center in this ad is a Fairlane Victoria hardtop coupe. For 1956, it gained a four-door hardtop sibling, Ford's first hardtop sedan.

Left: Thunderbirds got minor revisions for 1956. Most noticeable was a trunk-mounted spare tire, commonly called a "continental kit." Also, the optional hardtop gained its famous portholes, and front-fender vents were added just forward of the doors. Optional was Ford's new 312-cubic-inch V-8 with up to 225 horsepower.

Ever since station wagons went to all-steel construction in the early 1950s, sales had taken off: In Ford's case, they had increased nine-fold since the beginning of the decade. Ford wagons made up their own series and were offered in a variety of styles and trim levels, including two-doors, four-doors, and the wood-grained Country Squire. For 1956, prices ranged from $2185 to $2533.

An external spare tire freed up trunk space.

Lincoln was all new for 1956, being longer, lower, and wider. It also got 60 more horsepower, now 285, courtesy of an enlarged 368-cubic-inch V-8. Capri was now the entry model, Premiere the new top-line series. A Premiere four-door sedan went for $4601, a convertible for $4747.

A Premiere convertible, with new wraparound windshield, prominent rear fender ends, and hooded front wheel arches, à la Cadillac. Grillework was massive, but clean.

Added to the Ford Motor Company line for 1956 was the ultraluxury Continental Mark II. Offered only as a two-door coupe, it cost nearly $10,000—double that of a Lincoln. Inspired by the beautiful, low-slung, high-priced Lincoln Continentals of the '40s, it was likewise aimed at very discriminating (read "rich") buyers who appreciated distinctive styling, understated luxury, and exclusivity. And exclusive it was: Just 2556 were built for debut '56. Beneath the lengthy hood sat Lincoln's 285-horse-power 368-cubic-inch V-8. Ad writers took a rather unusual approach but perhaps knew their prospective buyers well, luring them with "the excitement of being conservative."

A classic long-hood/short-deck profile marked the Continental Mark II—Ford's brighter idea, attempting to recapture a major share of the high-end market. Their immodest goal: to create America's most luxurious, carefully crafted production car. Mechanical components were shared with Lincoln, but Continental began as a Ford division unto itself.

Tacky if installed on a lesser car, the simulated spare-tire bulge looked just right on a Continental coupe—reminiscent of 1940-48 ancestors.

New to the Mercury line for 1956 was a four-door hardtop body style shared with Ford. Also added was a new entry-level series called Medalist. The four-door hardtop shown in the foreground is a top-line $2835 Montclair, but it was also offered in the other three Mercury trim levels: Medalist, Custom, and Monterey.

Mercury styling didn't change much for 1956, though the cars did get a revised front bumper and altered side trim. This $2712 Custom convertible sports the optional continental kit, which moved the spare tire to the back bumper.

The least expensive '56 Mercury, a $2254 Medalist two-door sedan, shows off the limited chrome trim applied to this new entry-level series.

A Custom two-door sedan cost about $100 more than its "stripped" Medalist counterpart, but looked classier thanks to its extra chrome trim.

Though the station wagon body was shared with Ford, Mercury's was mounted on a longer wheelbase. The taillights on Merc wagons were unique to this body style, as they had to fit the same outline as those on the Ford version. This Custom listed for $2722 in six-passenger form, $2819 outfitted for eight passengers.

General Motors

Buicks got minor front and rear styling updates for 1956 along with a few more ponies for the 322-cubic-inch V-8, now with up to 255 hp. Those seeking open-air enjoyment with Buick luxury could find it in the $2740 Special convertible.

A top-line Roadmaster sedan listed for $3503. It was far outsold by its fancier four-door-hardtop sibling, which cost $189 more.

Wagons were offered as entry-level 220-hp Specials (shown) or hot-rod 255-hp Centurys. They cost $2775 and $3256, respectively.

Above: Cadillacs didn't look much different for 1956, and that included the high-end $6556 Eldorado convertible, which added "Biarritz" to its name. It was joined by a two-door-hardtop version called the Eldorado Seville, which cost the same.

Below: A smaller-mesh grille was the biggest front-end change to the '56 Caddy. But behind the grille sat an enlarged V-8 that grew from 331 cubic inches to 365, bringing with it 285 horses in base form, 305 in the Eldorado. The stately $5047 Sixty Special sedan rode a four-inch-longer wheelbase than its Series 62 counterpart, which partially explains its near-$800 price premium.

Tailfins wore flat tops for 1956, as shown on this $4624 Coupe de Ville. Joining it that year was a four-door hardtop called Sedan de Ville. Both names would continue to grace Cadillacs for decades to come.

Above: Chevrolet picked up the pace for 1956 with a mild facelift and more power: up to 225 horses from the 265-cubic-inch V-8. Ads proclaimed "The Hot One's Even Hotter." And indeed it was. Zora Arkus-Duntov, renowned for his work with the Corvette, set an American Stock Sedan record in the grueling Pikes Peak Hill Climb. His time of 17 minutes, 24 seconds beat the old record by a resounding two minutes. The top V-8 could be ordered in any '56 Chevy, including this entry-level 150 two-door sedan, yours (at the time) for just $1826.

Below: At the opposite end of the two-door spectrum was the Bel Air Sport hardtop at $2176.

Above: Most popular of the '56 Chevys was the midline 210 Series. And the most popular 210 was the $1955 four-door sedan.

Below: Among "regular" Chevrolets, the $2608 two-door Nomad wagon still topped the price ladder for 1956. To many, its sporty good looks made it worth the $126 it cost over and above a comparable four-door Bel Air wagon.

Chevy finally got on board the four-door hardtop train in '56 with the Sport hardtop sedan. Offered in 210 (shown) and fancier Bel Air trim, the hardtops cost $162 more than regular four-door pillared sedans. That put the 210 version at $2117, the Bel Air at $2230.

Corvette got a radical makeover for 1956 that likely spared its life. Not only did it look better, but the redesign brought expected features such as roll-up windows (the original had clumsy snap-in side curtains) and outside door handles (owners previously had to reach inside the car to open the latch). Newly optional were power windows, a power convertible top, and a detachable hardtop. Up to 225 horsepower was now offered, which didn't hurt, either. The price rose a bit to $3149, while sales rose fivefold to 3467.

The Corvette's bodyside coves permitted neat two-toning, which was a distinctive styling element that made the car instantly recognizable. They would last through the end of this styling generation in 1962.

Above: Less demanding was the Super 88 Holiday hardtop coupe at $2808.

Below: Oldsmobile's V-8 remained at 324 cubic inches for '56, but power rose from 202 horsepower to 240 in the Super 88 and this Ninety-Eight Holiday four-door hardtop sedan.

A large "loop" front bumper and revised side trim marked the 1956 Oldsmobiles, which otherwise hadn't changed much since '54. This was rather unusual for the time period, as annual styling changes were considered necessary to maintain sales. And indeed, Olds dropped back down to fifth in industry production. The line-topping Ninety-Eight Starfire convertible demanded $3740.

Right: The bed of the $3129 Safari two-door wagon had carpeting and chrome skid strips. Taillights were hooded linewide.

Below: Like Chevrolet, Pontiac belatedly added a four-door hardtop body style to its lineup for 1956. Shown is the top-line Star Chief version, which went for $2735.

Other Star Chief body styles included the $2665 Custom Catalina hardtop coupe.

Above: Pontiac sheetmetal was unchanged for '56, but grilles picked up additional chrome. Round parking lights flanked rocket-pod doodads, and the Star Chief "stars" were replaced with flattened ovals at the rear quarters.

Below: Four-door wagons shared rear fenders with Chevrolet wagons, and thus carried unique Chevy-shaped taillights. Offered only in the Chieftain series, this nine-passenger version cost $2653.

Studebaker-Packard Corporation

Clipper was made a separate make for 1956 and, having lost its Packard lineage, sales plummeted; ironic, because Clippers were now closer to the big Packards than ever before, as they no longer wore different taillights.

Clipper was replaced in the lineup by the Executive, which shared the Clipper's body but had a "big Packard" grille and a bit more power: Both had a 352-cubic-inch V-8, but the Executive's made 275 horsepower vs. 240 hp for the Clipper. Executive was offered only as a four-door sedan or hardtop coupe (both shown). At $3465 for the sedan and $3560 for the coupe, prices sat about $400 to $600 north of comparable Clippers, $600 to $700 south of the big Patrician sedan and Four Hundred hardtop. It should have been popular, but wasn't: The Executive accounted for fewer than 3000 sales.

Packard's big cars made a mild comeback for 1956, but it was too little too late. Tops among Packard's closed models was the $4190 Four Hundred hardtop coupe; the Patrician sedan cost $30 less. Both were powered by a new 374-cubic-inch V-8—the biggest in the industry— making 290 horsepower.

Still hanging on was the flamboyant Caribbean convertible, now joined by a hardtop version. Priced at $5995 and $5495, respectively, only about 270 of each were sold. Both carried a 310-hp version of the 374-cid V-8. These stately cars were the last of the "true" Packards, a sad but fitting farewell to a prestigious marque that had once been America's luxury leader.

Tri-toning was almost expected in the open Caribbean. Wire wheels, air, and Twin-Traction were the only options.

Presidents continued on their longer 120.5-inch wheelbase and were offered as two- and four-door sedans with prices ranging from $2188 to $2489.

Mainline Studebakers were redesigned for 1956. Still on the same wheelbases, ads claimed they were bigger— and they looked it. Top-line Presidents got a new 289-cid V-8 with 195-225 horsepower; Commanders kept a 259 with 170-185 hp, Champions a 185-cid six with 101. Wagons were available in each series under the names Pinehurst, Parkview, and Pelham. Also restyled were the long-wheelbase coupes, which got a new "gaping mouth" grille and small tailfins.

Right: Packard donated the big 352-cubic-inch 275-horsepower V-8 that was squeezed under the long hood of the newly named Golden Hawk—the top trim level of Studebaker's long-wheelbase coupes. Ads claimed the engine gave the Golden Hawk a "hurricane of power." Other versions of the coupe continued in hardtop and pillared forms with six-cylinder or 259/289-cid V-8 power under the names Flight Hawk, Power Hawk, and Sky Hawk.

Below: Just 4071 Golden Hawks were produced, with a $3061 price tag. A large square grille ahead of an elevated hood helped conceal its 1953-55 coupe origin.

The top-line Pinehurst wagon had a 289-cid V-8 and a $2529 price tag.

1957

Following 1956 sales, the auto industry managed a modest rebound for '57. But disaster loomed by year's end, as economic recessions knocked at the nation's door.

In this season of the tailfin, those oh-so-American rear-end appendages soared taller, but had not yet reached their zenith. American cars also began a switch to quad headlamps, but they were ruled illegal (temporarily) in several states. For that reason, several '57 makes can be found with either single or twin lights on each side.

Few realized its significance, but AMC was about to lead the way into the compact era, killing off its big cars in mid-season to concentrate solely on Ramblers. Chrysler products, meanwhile, drew raves for their overwhelming "Forward Look" shapes as well as new Torsion-Aire Ride.

Most domestic cars switched to 14-inch wheels, several offered six-way power seats, and luxury models came with electric door locks. In some cars, speedometer buzzers sounded when a preset speed was reached. Several had nonslip differentials.

Studebaker-Packard plopped a supercharger atop its V-8 engine—a hop-up device unseen since the final Kaisers, and far more potent this time around. Pontiac unleashed a Bonneville convertible, named for the desolate Utah salt flats where so many landspeed records were set and broken. Plusher and more powerful than any prior model, it helped set the stage for Pontiac's transformation into a performance-oriented marque.

The 42nd National Automobile Show, the first since 1940, was held at New York's new Coliseum in late 1956 to showcase the longer, lower '57 models. Vice President Nixon spoke at a banquet during the show—the first one to be televised.

An average car sold for $2749, whereas the average worker now earned $4230 yearly, and median family income neared $5000. Physicians topped $22,000, while teachers stood a little below the overall average. Factory workers might expect to pull in about $2.08 an hour.

The Soviet Union launched *Sputnik*, the first space satellite, into orbit, followed by *Sputnik II*, which carried a dog. America's

Viking satellite, meanwhile, exploded prior to takeoff at Cape Canaveral, Florida.

Despite popular acclaim for unceasing prosperity, a few critics had harsh words to say about the burgeoning consumer society. Director Martin Ritt made caustic observations of the suburban lifestyle in a little-noticed movie, *No Down Payment*.

All told, it was a fine year for Hollywood, with such critically acclaimed (and popular) features as *Twelve Angry Men*, *The Bridge on the River Kwai*, and *Gunfight at the O.K. Corral*. On a darker note, Andy Griffith shined as *A Face in the Crowd*, portraying a wastrel-turned-celebrity in this searing exposé of media-induced publicity.

Raymond Burr's *Perry Mason* appeared on TV for the first time. So did *Wagon Train* and *Leave It to Beaver*, along with James Garner in *Maverick*. Dick Clark launched *American Bandstand* to capture the attention of teenagers after school. Half of the top shows were westerns. Studios could now use videotape, heralding the demise of live television. The Everly Brothers sang "Bye, Bye Love," but their humorous ditty "Wake Up Little Susie" was banned in Boston. Jerry Lee Lewis noted that there was a "Whole Lot of Shaking Going On," as Little Richard belted out his tribute to "Lucille." Debbie Reynolds hit the pop charts with her rendition of "Tammy," and Harry Belafonte scored with the "Banana Boat Song."

Parents worried about a flu pandemic, while kids played with Slinky and Hula Hoops, and Sony issued a pocket-size transistor radio. Ford's director of engineering research warned that production of natural petroleum might "peak out" in the next two decades, but few believed that fuel supplies would ever be threatened.

One-third of new cars, according to a new study, were purchased by middle-class families, earning $5000 to $7500 per year. More than two-thirds of them were bought on credit. Not even the prospect of increased credit, though, would help the auto industry through the rocky economic seas that lay immediately ahead.

American Motors Corporation

Top: Nineteen fifty-seven would prove to be Hudson's last hurrah. The company greeted the model year with a mildly revised Hornet, now flying alone as the shorter Wasp departed the nest. Prices for the surviving V-8 models were lower, but entry-level prices were higher because the six-cylinder versions were history. Power came from a 327-cubic-inch V-8 rated at 255 horsepower—35 more than the top '56 engine. Styling changes were predictably minimal: taller tacked-on fins in back, dual tacked-on fins in front, and altered side trim. Total sales barely topped 4000 units, and, with that, the once proud Hudson nameplate bid the land adieu. It was a sad end for a company that just four years earlier had been the terror of the stock-car tracks.

Bottom: Added "V" motifs on the front and tacked-on tailfins marked 1957 Hudsons.

Mild trim shuffling improved the look of final Hudsons, but they still ranked as garish. Wasps were gone, leaving only a Hornet sedan and hardtop.

Above: Nash made a valiant effort to stay afloat with a surprisingly effective facelift for '57. Where it was legal, it boasted dual headlights a year before most makes adopted them. Nashes shared the 327 V-8 found in surviving Hudsons and likewise were reduced to a single model. Ambassador prices started at $2586—$235 less than Hornet's—but model-year production was even lower, at 3600. AMC saw the writing on the wall, put the bleeding Nash nameplate out of its misery, and staked the corporate future on the compact Rambler. Never again would a new Nash fold its seats to afford its owners a free night's sleep.

Right: AMC gambled its future on the proposition that Americans didn't want a "big, over-chromiumed rolling cabana" but would accept a frugal car if it were sufficiently roomy.

Above: Fully open front wheels, a revised grille, and quad headlamps marked Ambassador Customs and Supers.

Bottom Left: AMC chose to distance the Rambler from its failing linemates by making it a separate make for 1957; note the "R" on the hubcaps. Sales skyrocketed, led by the $2500 six-cylinder Custom Cross Country station wagon. Three-tone color combinations were offered, along with Rambler's first V-8, the 250-cubic-inch 190-horsepower engine fitted to late-'56 Ambassadors and Hornets.

But an even bigger V-8—the 327-cid engine used in the '57 Nashes and Hudsons—was stuffed into a Rambler to produce the hot-rod Rebel. Horsepower was raised from 255 to 270 for this application, and in the light, 3300-lb four-door hardtop, made for a "sleeper" road rocket that previewed the formula used by muscle cars of the next decade. Rebels were said to be quicker than every other '57 car but the Corvette.

Top: Painted light silver metallic, Rebels had a gold anodized aluminum sidespear.

Right: Also gaining its independence this year was the tiny English-built Metropolitan, which likewise got its own insignia on its hubcaps. And it likewise showed a big sales gain—from 7645 to 13,425—despite a slight price increase that set the coupe at $1567 and the convertible at $1591.

The Metro convertible ran $24 more than a hardtop. Both the Metro convertible and hardtop retained the little rear-mounted spare tire, and typically sported colorful two-toning.

Top Left: The second generation of Virgil Exner's Forward Look caused a sensation when the 1957 models hit showrooms. They indeed looked futuristic with their flowing lines and tall fins, and, where legal, many sported quad headlights. Not surprisingly, engines grew once again; the Hemi used in New Yorkers was now a 392 with 325 horsepower. Newly available was the three-speed TorqueFlite automatic transmission introduced the previous year on Imperials. Also new was torsion-bar front suspension. A New Yorker coupe went for $4202.

Top Right: The usual ad rhetoric notwithstanding, it's difficult to imagine such praise—"Most glamorous car in a generation"—being lavished on the boxy Chryslers of just three years before.

Above Left and Middle: Perhaps even more glamorous than the four-door sedan in the ad was this $4638 New Yorker convertible. Rear fins rose gracefully from the fendertops; dramatically backswept wheel arches imparted a sense of speed and forward movement. Oddly, just 1049 were sold.

Above Right: Chrysler's muscular 300-C (the letter suffix would take one step up the alphabet every year) got a unique grille for '57 rather than sharing it with the Imperial. As with other 1957 Chryslers, the 300 was long, slim, and sculptured, yet relatively restrained in its decoration. A convertible was offered for the first time, yet drew only 484 orders at its steep $5359 starting price.

Faring even worse saleswise was the 300's counterpart over at sister division DeSoto. Built on the same size wheelbase, the Adventurer had to "make do" with 345 hp from a 345-cubic-inch Hemi. A mere 300 convertible versions were sold at $4272—more than a grand less than a comparable 300-C.

Firesweep was DeSoto's lowest trim level, but you wouldn't know it by the look of this $3169 Shopper station wagon. It could be ordered with a rear-facing third-row seat.

Above: Non-Adventurer DeSotos got the front-end treatment of this Firesweep coupe; the example shown has the dual headlights still required in some states for the '57 model year. Firesweeps had a 325-cubic-inch V-8 with up to 260 horsepower, Firedome and Fireflite a 341 with up to 290 hp.

Right: This Coronet Lancer coupe started at $2580, but was optioned with the top D-500 engine, a 354 Hemi V-8 with 340 hp. Interiors held a pushbutton TorqueFlite selector, dashboard-mounted mirror, pull-handle parking brake, and Scope-Sight speedometer above a full bank of gauges.

To distinguish them from lesser DeSotos, Adventurers wore a headlight treatment similar to that used on the Chrysler 300-C. The coupe version cost $3997 and sold 1650 copies.

"Swept-Wing" styling graced Dodges for 1957. A six-cylinder engine was still offered, but few Dodges were purchased that way; most had a 325-cid V-8 with up to 310 hp.

Dodge prices started at $2370 for a six-cylinder two-door sedan; fitting it with a V-8 cost $108 more. Like all '57 Chrysler Corp. cars, torsion-bar front suspension was standard, a three-speed TorqueFlite automatic transmission optional.

Right: For 1957, Imperial got its first distinct bodyshell; previously, it shared one with Chrysler models. Incorporated in the design was the first use of curved side glass in an American car. Not incorporated, but available as an option, was a fake spare tire cover for the trunklid. It proved popular, but in later years would be derided as the "toilet seat." Gun sight taillights remained, but were now set into the trailing edges of tall fins. A Crown convertible started at $5598.

Bottom: A Crown four-door—whether in hardtop or sedan form—went for $5406. Crown was the midline series now, LeBaron being installed as the top-line model.

Filling out the range of body styles offered is this $5269 Crown Southampton coupe. All Imperials came with the same 325-horsepower 392 Hemi used in most Chryslers.

Above: A $2638 Belvedere convertible shows off the year's revised dashboard.

Left: Topping the Plymouth line was again the white-hot Fury, again offered in only one color combination. New, however, was a 318-cid V-8 with 290 hp.

Bottom: A Belvedere four-door hardtop cost $109 more than a comparable four-door sedan, but many felt the sleeker look well worth the money. The 277-cubic-inch V-8 returned, but was joined by a 301-cid version with up to 235 horsepower.

Ford Motor Company

Set your family 2-Ford free

Ask to Action Test the new kind of FORD

Left: Ford's advertising encouraged buyers to pick up "two fine Fords for the price of one fine car." This ad shows a family that took the bait, allowing "the men" to go fishing in a $2451 Ford Country Sedan station wagon, while "she's free as the breeze" in a flashy $2281 Fairlane 500 coupe. Maybe the strategy worked: In 1957, Ford beat Chevrolet in the production race, a feat it would manage only twice during the decade.

Below: The finlets were a little more subdued on the Country Sedan station wagon, the core of Ford's strength in the wagon market.

Above: Fairlanes and Fairlane 500s featured fins that sprang from midbody.

Right: Some of Ford's success that year may have been attributable to the fact the completely restyled '57 Ford was going up against a merely facelifted Chevy. A glamorous Fairlane 500 Sunliner convertible shows off Ford's sleek new lines that incorporated pronounced tailfins. It could have been yours for $2505. Another $437 would have bought Ford's new Skyliner convertible with its retractable hardtop. The top Ford engine remained a 312-cubic-inch V-8, now with 245 horsepower, up 30 from '56.

Above: Speaking of sleek new lines, the Thunderbird was also updated for 1957, with similar "blade" tailfins topping a longer rear deck. Front ends wore a cleaner grille, and the combination resulted in what was perhaps the best-looking of the two-seat T-Birds—and also the last. Horsepower of the 312-cid V-8 rose to as much as 285, with a supercharged version weighing in at a rousing 340.

Top Right: Thick, thin, and even horizontal fins were drawn up in the quest for ideas for the '57 Thunderbird.

Bottom Left: The limited-edition $10,000 Continental Mark II became even more limited for 1957, as only 444 copies were sold—down from 2556 the year before. Though the name would live on, 1957 would be the final year for this classic design.

Bottom Right: Lincoln got a fresh face for 1957, though it differed little except for new stacked quad headlights. Prices rose significantly, the top-line Premiere convertible now commanding $5381.

Above: Ford also introduced the Ranchero for 1957, basically a two-door station wagon with the rear cargo area replaced by a pickup bed. This concept resulted in what the ad called "the sleekest pickup ever to pack a load," and would be copied two years later by Chevy's El Camino.

Above: Lincoln tailfins grew up and out for '57, becoming much more prominent. Also more prominent was the price of this Premiere two-door hardtop, which now stood at $5149.

Below: Few cars changed more drastically for '57 than the redesigned Mercury. Heavy "eyebrows" over quad headlights distinguished the front, while the rear hosted channeled tailfins culminating in canted, U-shaped taillights. The cars looked far larger than their predecessors, and they were: Wheelbase was up by three inches on all versions. Model names were shuffled, too. Monterey was now the cheapest, followed by Montclair and the new Turnpike Cruiser. Prices ranged from $2576 to $4103.

Wagons now had their own series, and offered hardtop versions with two or four doors and prices from $2903 to $3677.

Above Left and Right: Newly installed at the top of the 1957 Mercury line was the chrome-bedecked Turnpike Cruiser. It was offered in only three body styles: convertible and two- or four-door hardtop. Hardtops featured a power-retractable reverse-slant rear window not shared with any other Mercury that year. Standard on the 'Cruiser was a new 290-horsepower 368-cubic-inch V-8, which was optional on other Mercs in place of a 255-horse 312. This Turnpike Cruiser two-door hardtop cost a princely $3758.

Right: A Turnpike Cruiser convertible—complete with spare tire continental kit in back—paced the 1957 running of the Indianapolis 500.

General Motors

Below: A Century wasn't Buick's lowest-priced convertible, but it was certainly its fastest. At $3598, it cost $600 more than its Special counterpart, and about $500 less than a Roadmaster ragtop.

Above: Buicks looked longer and lower for 1957, especially on the long-wheelbase chassis shared by the top-line Roadmaster (coupe shown) and midline Super. A larger 364-cubic-inch V-8 powered all Buicks that year. As had become tradition, the Roadmaster and the shorter, lighter, hot-rod Century got more power than other models: For 1957, that meant 300 horses vs. 250 for the Super and price-leading Special. Those figures were up by 45 and 30, respectively, over 1956. Buick prices ranged from $2596 for a Special two-door sedan to $4483 for the top Roadmaster four-door hardtop.

Right: The Century line also hosted the sporty new Caballero four-door hardtop wagon. It was Buick's best-selling wagon in '57, despite the fact its $3706 price made it by far the most expensive.

Below: These cowboys (and girls) seem to admire the room, comfort, power, and class afforded by a $3354 Century Riviera hardtop sedan.

Magnificent Beyond All Expectations!

Cadillac

Left: Cadillacs received a long-overdue redesign for 1957 that faithfully followed the "longer, lower, wider" mantra that prevailed during the decade—though it wasn't to the extreme depicted by the illustration in this ad. If the tail treatment looks familiar, it should: The high-end Eldorados had been wearing something very similar since '55.

Below: Front ends changed dramatically as well, though were still recognizable as Cadillacs. Most prices rose about $400-$700, bringing this Coupe de Ville in at $5116.

Below: In order to retain a unique identity—and justify their higher prices—Eldorados again displayed distinctive rear styling, with sharklike fins protruding from a sloping decklid. The convertible retained its Biarritz surname, the coupe its Seville suffix. Added (but not shown here) was a Seville four-door hardtop. All these Eldos carried the same $7286 base price.

If these Eldorados weren't sufficiently exclusive (read "expensive") for you, perhaps the new Eldorado Brougham would fill the bill—if indeed you could handle a bill that totaled a stratospheric $13,074. For that you got a specially built body with "suicide" rear doors, brushed stainless-steel roof, and quad headlights, along with an air-spring suspension and the virtual assurance you wouldn't see another car like yours on the road.

Right: For 1957, Chevrolet introduced what would become one of the most iconic cars of the Fifties. Though actually just a facelift of the '56 (itself a facelift of the '55), the '57 Chevy was a landmark design that still looks good today.

Below: One of the highlights of the year was a fuel-injected version of Chevy's newly enlarged 283-cubic-inch V-8 that produced up to 283 horsepower—the revered "one horsepower per cubic inch." Chrysler had done it the year before with the Hemi-powered 300-B, but that was a high-priced car that cost twice as much as the average Chevy. The "fuelie" engine was available on all models, including this bare-bones 150 utility sedan that started at just $1885.

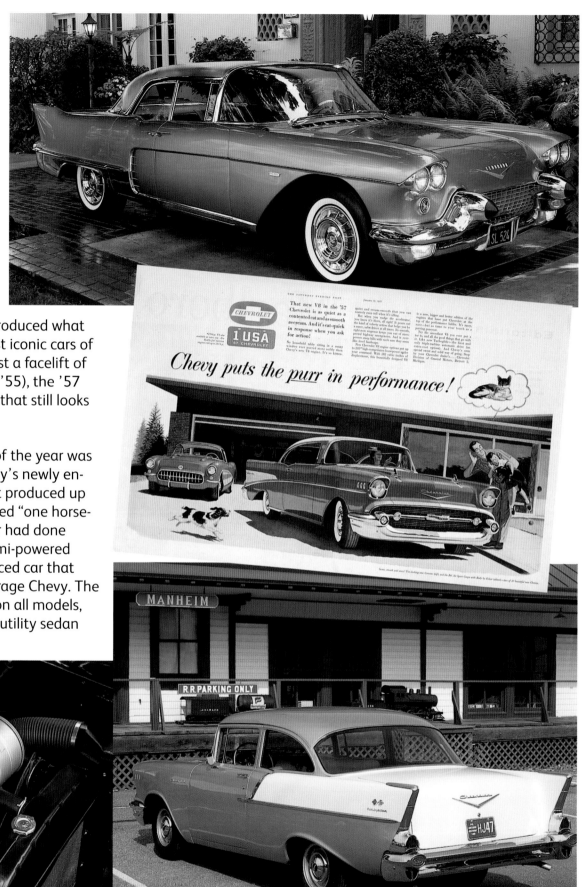

Pontiacs got revised styling for '57 that gave them rear-slanted tailfins and a sleeker, more modern look, as evidenced by this $3481 Star Chief Safari two-door hardtop wagon. Sadly, it would prove to be the final year for this attractive body style.

One of the most popular '57 Chevys was the top-line $2290 Bel Air four-door sedan.

Corvette looked little different for '57, but all engines gained power and a newly optional four-speed manual transmission made better use of it. A four-speed '57 fuelie—such as the one shown—was a formidable street car that was equally at home on a racetrack.

Studebaker-Packard Corporation

Above: Before the so-called "Packardbakers" of 1957-58 came to market, a more ambitious plan was in the works for 1957. Projectile headlight pods, swoopy tailfins, and dramatic wheel openings adorn this Clipper rendering by J. Ewart from October '55.

Right: The proposed '57 Clipper would have looked nothing like the Packards being considered for the year.

Packards moved to a body shared with Studebaker for 1957, and were built alongside them in Studebaker's factory in South Bend, Indiana. Styling was similar, though Packards carried their signature cathedral taillights. Packard's lineup was trimmed to just the four-door Town Sedan and the four-door Country Sedan, actually a station wagon—Packard's first since 1950. They were priced at $3212 and $3384, respectively, placing the sedan between the former Clipper and Packard Executive. Furthermore, both stood about $700 north of comparable Studebakers. The only engine was a supercharged version of Studebaker's 289-cubic-inch V-8 rated at 275 horsepower. Of course, these were Packards in name only, and sales dwindled to just 3940 sedans and 869 wagons.

Had finances allowed, the 1957-58 Packards might have matched Chrysler Corporation's low, lean look. Instead, the final Packards were tarted-up Studebakers. The '57 Clipper was designed by Dick Teague to share a bodyshell with the Studebaker President.

Left: Studebaker's redesigned 1957 mainstream models weren't nearly the flop that Packard's were. Meanwhile, the long-wheelbase Loewy coupes grew tailfins, and the line was reduced to just the top V-8-only Golden Hawk hardtop coupe and six-cylinder and V-8 Silver Hawk pillared coupe.

Below: Silver Hawks started at $2142 with a six-cylinder engine, $2263 with a 289-cubic-inch V-8. That was little more than a midline Chevrolet two-door sedan, so it's strange that only 15,000 of the sporty Silver Hawks were ever sold.

With Packard no longer building the big 352- cubic-inch 275-horsepower V-8 that so briskly propelled the Golden Hawk in 1956, Studebaker's beautiful hardtop coupe had to look elsewhere for power in '57. What it found was another Packard engine—or at least, another engine used in Packards. Actually, it was Studebaker's own 289-cid V-8 fitted with a Paxton supercharger, which resulted in the same 275 hp—and 100 pounds less weight. Ads claimed it provided "extra power the instant you need it."

Studebaker's station wagons had previously come only in two-door form, but the '57 redesign brought four-door versions as well. The top four-door wagon was the $2666 Broadmoor. Once again, Studebakers were offered with a choice of 185-cid/101-horsepower six, or 259/289-cid V-8s with 180-225 hp.

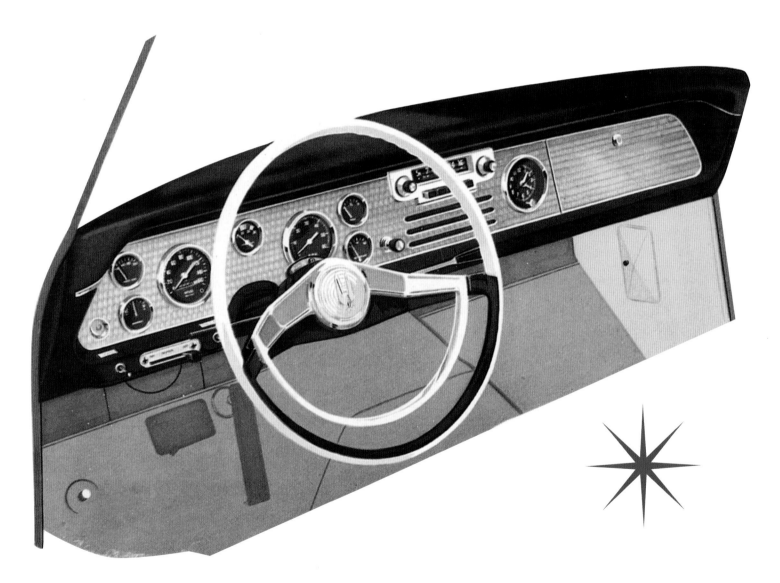

Aside from being Studebaker's only hardtop coupe, Golden Hawks could be identified by a long bulge in their hoods. Inside, round gauges set in an engine-turned dash panel befitting the car's sporty nature. Priced at $3182, only 4356 Golden Hawks were sold.

1958

Recession arrived with a vengeance to the shock and dismay of Americans who'd grown accustomed to prosperity. Inflation dipped below two percent, but unemployment approached and passed the seven-percent barrier. By June, 5,437,000 Americans were out of work—the highest figure since 1941.

Not that everyone was suffering. Those fortunate enough to have a full-time job might expect average earnings of $3851 per year. College teachers averaged $6015, and factory workers approached the $5000 mark. Dentists averaged more than $14,000, and the median family income reached $5087. Car prices rose 3.3 percent as the model year began, but the average amount paid for a new car actually dropped—to $2990, from $3230 a year earlier.

In the wake of Congressional hearings, the Automobile Information Disclosure Act was passed. From now on, window stickers would have to display every new vehicle's serial number and suggested retail price. Ever since, these documents have been known informally as "Monroney" stickers,

after the U.S. senator largely responsible for the new law.

Nearly all cars were bigger and heavier (though use of aluminum grew 13 percent). Chrysler adopted compound-curve windshields that reached into the roofline. That worked fine, but their new fuel-injected engines did not. Practically all makes adopted quad-headlamp setups, and horsepower ratings rose an average of seven percent (20 bhp).

The biggest news of the year was the arrival of the Edsel, Ford's great hope for the mid-price field. The excitement, however, would be short-lived; in this recession era, yet another rather costly car just couldn't attract enough customers to survive.

Over at General Motors, this year's Buicks and Oldsmobiles were branded the most gaudy and garish vehicles of the year—if not the decade or the century. Chevrolets, on the other hand, exhibited a graceful restyling, led by the posh Impala—with an available hot new Turbo Thrust engine.

Packard departed after a last-ditch attempt to stay afloat by gussying up their

Studebaker-based bodies even further. Henceforth, Studebaker would focus on its compact Lark, ready for market ahead of shrunken rivals from the Big Three.

George Romney turned AMC's full attention to compacts, including a revived reduced-size American. Still, many industry leaders echoed the thoughts of an anonymous GM executive: "If the public wants to lower its standard of living by driving a cheap crowded car, we'll make it."

Alaska became the forty-ninth state. America's first satellite was launched from Cape Canaveral, and the Soviets countered with *Sputnik III*.

Economist John Kenneth Galbraith, in *The Affluent Society*, criticized the conformity and materialism of Americans. John Keats published *The Insolent Chariots*, a devastating but comic critique of the auto trade and car culture.

Elvis Presley was drafted into the U.S. Army. Folk music, after trailing far behind rock 'n' roll and jazz in popularity, began a resurgence, led by the Kingston Trio's recording of "Tom Dooley."

The Donna Reed Show appeared on TV, along with Chuck Connors in *The Rifleman*. So did *77 Sunset Strip*. In a major scandal, quiz-show contestants pleaded guilty to having received answers ahead of time.

Moviegoers could see everything from Alfred Hitchcock's *Vertigo* to *Auntie Mame* and *Cat on a Hot Tin Roof*. Kim Stanley turned in a devastating performance as a movie queen in *The Goddess*, while Robert Mitchum drove hard through mountain roads as a whiskey runner in *Thunder Road*. Weekly movie admissions dipped below 40 million, the lowest figure since 1922—evidence of TV's impact.

Connie Francis sang "Who's Sorry Now," Peggy Lee belted out "Fever," and records could be played in stereo. Van Cliburn became the first American to win the top classical-music competition in Moscow.

Even though compacts were in the works at each Big Three auto company, the threat from such *sub*-compacts as the Volkswagen Beetle and Renault Dauphine was deemed insignificant. The era of big barges had a few more years to go, and Detroit had another season of excess on the drawing board.

American Motors Corporation

Slow sales of the "Hash"—a derisive term for the Hudson/Nash vehicles—convinced AMC Chairman George Romney to place the company's emphasis on the 108-inch-wheelbase Rambler.

AMC president George Romney had neither time nor money to come up with an all-new design, but Americans arrived at an opportune moment: during a recession, as imports were capturing serious sales.

Above Left: Several styling models of the developing long-wheelbase Rambler sedan and wagon bodies wore Hudson badges.

Above Right: With Hudson and Nash relegated to history, AMC could focus its development dollars on the Rambler, which sprouted fins and got a facelift for 1958. Wheelbase remained at 108 inches and the basic body structure carried over, but the look was all new. The 195-cubic-inch six returned as the standard engine. A revised 250-cid V-8 gained 25 horsepower for a total of 215, and all models so equipped were called "Rebel V-8." Sadly, their namesake—the hot-rod '57 Rebel—was dropped. The attraction of Rambler's fuel economy is evident in the fact the vast majority sold were powered by the six-cylinder engine.

Despite its compact pretensions, the Rambler was touted as a six-passenger vehicle. Although ads proclaimed they could be "six big 6-footers with their hats on," half a dozen folks who were small and very friendly would have been a more comfortable fit. Wagons drew the most advertising attention—and the most sales.

Above and Left: Effectively replacing the departed Hudson and Nash in AMC's line was a new Ambassador. Borrowing the name of Nash's former top trim level, it was an upscale version of the Rambler built on a longer wheelbase. Power came from the 327-cubic-inch V-8 formerly used in the hot '57 Rebel.

The hardtop station wagon was unique to the Ambassador line and the most expensive model at $3116; other Ambassadors were priced about $250 upstream of comparable Rambler V-8s. Four Ambassador body styles accounted for 14,862 sales, double that of the final Hudson and Nash combined—which still isn't saying much.

Ambassadors rode a 117-inch wheelbase, versus 108 inches for regular Ramblers. Stretching the body helped enhance the car's proportions. The tailgate flipped open to reveal a carpeted, padded cargo compartment. Despite the company's "economy" image, Rambler pushed the Ambassador as a luxury model.

Above: In a fortuitous move, AMC president George Romney brought out a smaller Rambler just as the nation was falling into a recession. Christened the American, it wasn't actually new: He merely dusted off the dies last used to stamp out 1955 Nash Rambler coupes. The 100-inch-wheelbase American was offered only as a two-door, yet sold more than 30,000 copies in its inaugural year—and it would go up from there. Prices started at just $1775, no doubt an important element in its resounding success. Due to the recession, every major automaker saw a sales decline for 1958 except for Rambler—whose sales doubled.

Right: Still being offered was the tiny Metropolitan, with an 85-inch wheelbase and a starting price of $1626.

Above Left: A 1958 recession hit the little-changed Chryslers pretty hard. The company fought back with a "spring special" Windsor Dartline, but in the end, Chrysler sales totaled about half those of 1957.

Above Right: The production '58 New Yorker actually had less side trim than the '57 model.

Above: Grilles were altered slightly, taillight lenses were shorter, and most engines gained a few horsepower, but Chrysler offered little new for '58 to entice buyers.

Right: The letter series took its usual step up the alphabetical ladder, but the 300-D was a virtual rerun of the 300-C.

DeSotos changed even less than their Chrysler siblings for '58, and quite predictably, sales dropped even more. A boost in engine displacement from 325/341 cubic inches to 350/361 cid probably didn't help during recessionary '58, when fuel economy suddenly became a concern—enough so to encourage the Big Three to develop the compacts that would appear for 1960. As it turned out, it marked the beginning of the end for poor DeSoto.

A DeSoto Adventurer two-door hardtop started at $4071, but the convertible commanded $298 more. This hardtop has rare spinner hubcaps and gold-fleck carpeting. All DeSotos got a more complex grille.

Stacked taillights made DeSotos easy to spot. Only 3243 Fireflite Sportsman four-door hardtops were built, starting at $3731. The 361-cid V-8 developed 305 horsepower. Note the curiously pinched exhaust outlets.

In an odd reversal of recent trends, the hot-rod D-500 option actually lost horsepower for '58 (gasp!) thanks to a switch from a 354 Hemi V-8 to a less efficient—but cheaper—361 "wedge-head." The top-rated engine dropped seven hp to 333.

Faring slightly better was Dodge, which though also little-changed, still offered a frugal six-cylinder engine—and, of course, lower prices. With little else to tout, a "New Spring Swept-Wing" was released midyear with "Breathtaking new colors" and "Bewitching new interiors."

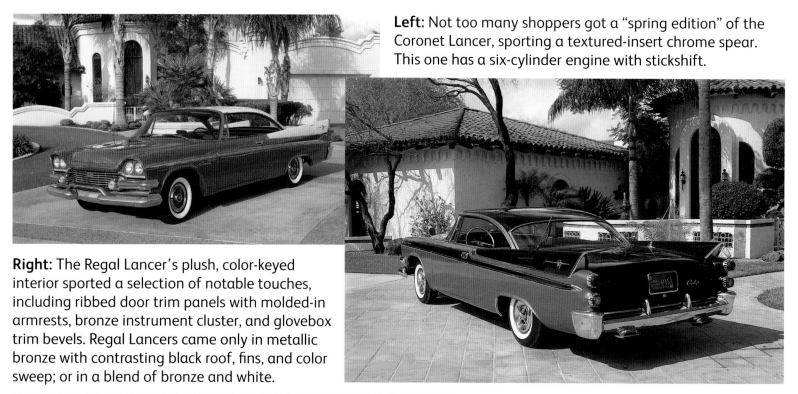

Left: Not too many shoppers got a "spring edition" of the Coronet Lancer, sporting a textured-insert chrome spear. This one has a six-cylinder engine with stickshift.

Right: The Regal Lancer's plush, color-keyed interior sported a selection of notable touches, including ribbed door trim panels with molded-in armrests, bronze instrument cluster, and glovebox trim bevels. Regal Lancers came only in metallic bronze with contrasting black roof, fins, and color sweep; or in a blend of bronze and white.

If you liked the 1957 Imperial, you'd probably like the '58 as well. In fact, you'd probably be hard-pressed to tell them apart. In what was otherwise a nearly standpat year, horsepower rose by 20, prices by about $100. This Crown two-door hardtop went for $5388.

Top: For '58, Imperial side trim remained restrained; Exner's aerodynamic "wedge" profile was thought not to need excessive adornment.

Above: Though the flashier hardtop sedan cost the same, about a third of four-door buyers bought the traditional pillared sedan. In the midline Crown series, it cost $5632.

Left: Though "new" appears four times in this ad copy, there really wasn't much that was on 1958 Plymouths. An exception was a larger 350-cubic-inch V-8 optional on all models (instead of just the top-line Fury coupe) that made 305 horsepower, or 315 with the very rare—and rather unreliable—fuel injection.

Below: The Belvedere line offered Plymouth's classiest hardtop sedan for $2528. Whether two doors or four, hardtops cost about $70-$90 more than comparable pillared bodies.

Bottom: The most popular Plymouth of all was the $2305 Savoy four-door sedan. Engine choices ranged from a thrifty 230-cubic-inch six to the hot-rod fuelie 350, but most were probably sold with a 318-cid V-8 of 225-250 hp.

Ford Motor Company

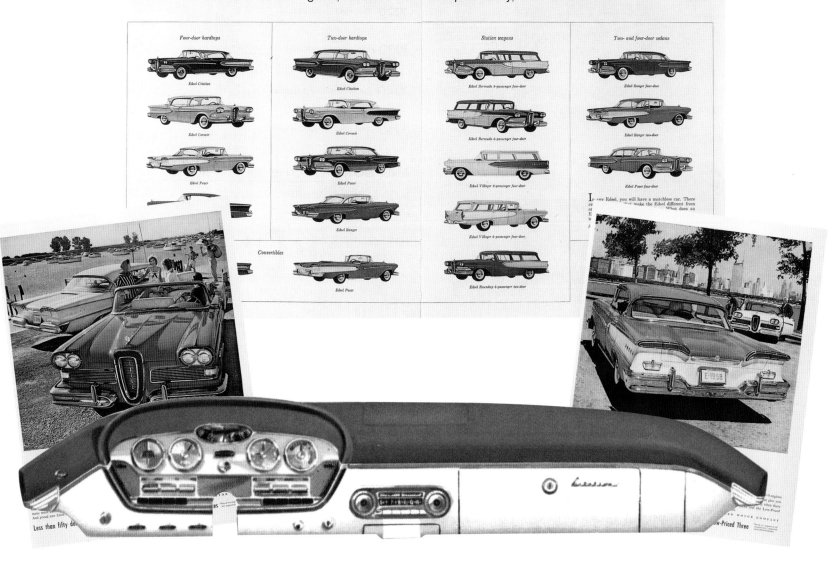

This is the **EDSEL**

"The same air of elegance, the same look of superb ability, in all its 18 models"

An attempt to bridge the growing price gap between Ford and Mercury resulted in the 1958 introduction of the infamous Edsel. Named after Henry Ford II's older brother, who met an untimely death in 1943, none at the time could have known that "Edsel" would later become a synonym for "failure." But a failure it most certainly was, though not necessarily at first. In fact, it was in many ways a fine automobile—a fine automobile killed by a grille that would have looked more at home in the '30s. Oddly, the rear view was modern and attractive, with rear-fender coves and thin horizontal taillights. It wasn't until buyers saw a grille that looked as though it had been caught sucking a lemon that they turned away. But it didn't turn them all away, at least not in the beginning. Offered in a vast array of body styles and trim variations, more than 63,000 Edsels were sold that first year, which, though far below expectations, wasn't a horrible showing.

Above Left: Edsels were offered in four series on two wheelbases: The shorter was shared with some Ford models, the longer was close to Mercury dimensions. The latter held the Corsair and top-line Citation, which were powered by a 345-horsepower 410-cubic-inch V-8. Shown is a $3535 Citation two-door hardtop, which carried a Mercury-like roofline.

Above Right: Ranger and Pacer rode the shorter Edsel chassis and got a 303-hp 361-cid V-8. This $2805 Pacer two-door hardtop sports a roofline similar to that used on Ford hardtops.

Upper Left: Edsel offered Ranger and Pacer two- and four-door wagons that were based on those from sister division Ford. Edsel's wagon prices ranged from $2876 to $3247.

Lower Left: Fords got a facelift for 1958, which brought quad headlights above a heavier grille and quad oval taillights. The top-line Fairlane 500 line offered two convertibles: the conventional Sunliner and the retractable-hardtop Skyliner. The Sunliner was priced at $2650.

Bottom Left: Production of Ford's Fairlane 500 Skyliner retractable hardtop coupe dropped to 14,713 cars, priced at $3163.

Also in the Fairlane family was the $2435 Victoria hardtop coupe. A hardtop sedan was offered as well, along with pillared versions of each.

Inside the '58 Ford brochure was information on the new 332- and 352-cubic-inch V-8s that supplanted the previous 312. Available horsepower ranged from 205 to a stout 300.

Above: Ford two- and four-door wagons again had their own series. Shown is the least expensive of them, the $2397 two-door Ranch Wagon.

Below: Thunderbird gained a new look and a rear seat in a radical 1958 redesign. Now a four-seater, the "Square Bird," as it became known, gained 11 inches in wheelbase and 800 lbs of weight. Convertible prices were up about $500 to $3929.

A $3631 coupe was added to the line and promptly took the vast majority of sales—by a 16:1 margin. The only engine offered this year was the 300-horsepower 352-cubic-inch V-8 available in regular Fords.

Right: If Mercury took the "Most Changed" crown for 1957, Lincoln likely earned it for '58. Where before Lincolns looked big and sleek, they now looked square and massive. Buyers evidently didn't like the change; prices were up only slightly, but sales dropped by 58 percent. Capri and Premiere series returned, both powered by a new 430-cubic-inch 375-horsepower V-8. A Premiere Landau hardtop sedan cost $5505.

Bottom: A change in philosophy made the once-exclusive Continental—now christened the Mark III—a gussied-up Lincoln at about $500 more. Offerings expanded to include a two-door hardtop, four-door hardtop and sedan, and this $6283 convertible, a body style no longer offered as a Lincoln. Though it watered down the Continental name, sales increased 28-fold.

Above: Mercury styling was revised for 1958, but the biggest news was under the hood: Optional was Lincoln's 430-cubic-inch V-8—the largest engine sold in America—with up to 400 horsepower. Also new was a pushbutton transmission selector. This Montclair Turnpike Cruiser coupe cost $3498.

Below: Hardtop wagons were in their sophomore year, priced from $3035 to $3775.

Above: A Continental Mark III convertible faces the line-up offered at Lincoln-Mercury dealers for 1958.

Below: The new top-line Mercury for '58 was the Park Lane, which rode a longer wheelbase than other models. A four-door-hardtop version cost $3944.

Above: Uniquely trimmed—but no less conspicuous—was the top-line Limited hardtop coupe at $5002.

Buick went baroque in 1958 with an ornate grille housing 160 shiny squares, along with pointed tailfins overlaying gaudy chrome side panels. To many, this was just too much, even for the flashy Fifties. Surely a blinding sight when the sun was shining, this Roadmaster convertible went for $4680.

Below: Cadillacs weren't exactly wallflowers themselves for 1958, gaining taller, pointed tailfins and the quad headlamps worn by most every car that year. This Series 62 convertible cost $5454.

For another $2000, a buyer could opt for the specialty Eldorado convertible with the same unique tailfins it wore for '57. Only 815 folks anted up the extra cash.

A long-wheelbase $6232 Cadillac Sixty Special would take a back seat to nobody in a contest of chrome.

Upper Right: One of those "lesser models" was the regular Bel Air. In two-door-sedan form, it cost $200 less than a comparable Impala. Joining the 235-cubic-inch six and 283-cid V-8 for '58 was a new 348-cid V-8. This "big-block" (as opposed to the "small-block" 283) was a converted truck engine, and offered from 250 to 315 horsepower.

Lower Right: For 1958, Chevy's former entry-level 150 series was renamed Delray, a moniker previously used on a midline 210 coupe. Two-door Delray sedans such as this one started as low as $2013. Replacing the midline 210 was the Biscayne, which—model for model—cost about $135 more than a Delray.

Bottom: Corvette adopted quad-headlight styling for 1958, which also brought a revised grille. Unique to this model year were slotted hood vents and dual chrome trunklid spears, easy ways to tell a '58 from any other model. The popularity of Chevy's sports car was growing every year, and even a substantial price hike for '58 didn't slow that down. At $3631, a Corvette cost nearly $800 more than the most expensive Impala convertible.

A drastic redesign greeted Chevy buyers for 1958. Newly installed as the top-line model that year was the Impala, technically a subseries of the Bel Air line. It was offered only as a convertible or a hardtop coupe, shown here. In V-8 form, they were priced at $2841 and $2693, respectively. Six-cylinder versions cost about $100 less. Note the three taillights on each side that, during the 1960s, would come to signify an Impala; lesser models had one or two.

Top: A solid contender for the King of Bling in '58 was the redesigned Oldsmobile—especially in top-line Ninety-Eight trim. This chrome-encrusted convertible cost $4300. Underhood, the available J-2 engine option for the 371-cubic-inch V-8 now yielded 312 horsepower.

Right: Sharing the Ninety-Eight's glitzy trim was the Super 88, which rode a 3.3-inch-shorter wheelbase. It's represented here by the $3529 convertible.

Bottom: Not quite as blindingly bright was the base Olds, newly named Dynamic 88. This Holiday hardtop coupe cost $2893.

The Super 88 Fiesta hardtop wagon was a fast and flashy hauler at $3623.

Below: Pontiacs received a total makeover for 1958, and like its GM siblings, piled on the chrome. Nowhere was this more evident than in the top-line Bonneville, which now rode the shorter Chieftain wheelbase and added a two-door hardtop to the existing convertible. A monumental $2200 price cut put the convertible at $3586; the coupe cost $3481.

Upper Right: Pontiac's new quad-headlight front end took center stage, but also new was that all models got the 370-cubic V-8 previously reserved for Bonnevilles. It produced from 240 to 300 horsepower, or 310 in Bonneville's fuel-injected version. A Bonneville convertible (shown) paced that year's Indy 500.

Lower Right: Safari station wagons appeared in the low-line Chieftain and top-line Star Chief series. Only the Chieftain offered a third-row seat. This Star Chief Safari went for $3350, about $330 more than a comparable Chieftain.

Studebaker-Packard Corporation

Right: Packard tried—perhaps a bit too hard—to project a fresh face for 1958. Quad headlights (adopted by nearly all 1958 cars) and a wide-mouth grille were surrounded by housings that appeared to be tacked on, though a sloping hood with built-in scoop was an aesthetic plus. Brochures called the new look "the most original styling on the road." Indeed. Mainstream Packards lost the supercharged engine they gained in '57, using instead a nonsupercharged Studebaker 289 with 210 horsepower.

Below: Rarest of the 1958 Packards—which were pretty rare in any form—was the $3384 wagon.

Added to the line was this svelte $3262 two-door hardtop, but it hardly helped sales, as just 675 were built.

Top: Also new was the Hawk hardtop coupe, which was pretty obviously just a Studebaker Golden Hawk made to look as though it was trying to swallow a frisbee. It was the only Packard to use the supercharged 289 V-8, as did the Golden Hawk. As such, the Hawk's lofty $3995 sticker—a mighty $710 more than a Golden Hawk—attracted just 588 buyers. All told, Packard sold just 2622 cars for 1958, and finally decided to throw in the towel—about two years too late.

Right: Studebaker's 1958 restyle looked quite good—if you were far enough away not to notice the tacked-on quad headlight bezels shared with Packards. A wrap-around grille was topped by a more upright hood (carried over from '57), that ads claimed "combine to impart a high-fashion elegance."

Above: Also shared with Packard was this rakish two-door hardtop body style, called the Starlight. Available in Commander (with 259-cubic-inch V-8) and top-line President trim (shown here, with 289-cid V-8), they sold for $2493 and $2695, respectively.

Left: Other mainstream Studebakers wore what ads called "Hawk-inspired body styling," and should have sold better than they did. They would prove to be the last of these larger cars Studebaker would build.

Right: Golden Hawks, still with a supercharged 289-cubic-inch V-8, sold just 878 copies for 1958. Silver Hawks did much better and would live on, but the Golden Hawk name would fly no more.

Bottom: A surprising 1958 hit for Studebaker was the no-frills Scotsman, which wore the '57 front end and an amazingly modest amount of chrome—this was the Fifties, after all. Offered as two- and four-door sedans and a two-door wagon, they sold for $1795 to $2055, about $380 less than comparable Champions.

1959

If any year serves as the consummate example of Fifties immoderation, it has to be 1959.

Cadillac tailfins reached as tall as they ever would, and virtually every other make's stretched only a little shorter. Ignoring the troubles GM had experienced with air suspensions, Chrysler launched its own version this year. Studebaker dropped the hot Golden Hawk but issued a more modest Silver Hawk coupe.

After arriving on the market with such promise and potential a year earlier, Edsel was already on the ropes. A handful of 1960 models were issued, built late this year; after which the name survived only as a virtual synonym for mammoth failure. Engines continued to grow in size and strength as the horsepower race wore on. Chrysler abandoned the legendary Hemi V-8 engine but had a selection of wedge-chambered powerhouses to take its place.

Pontiac went "Wide-Track," and Chevrolet added four-door models to the top Impala lineup. Ford launched a Galaxie to rival the Impala, while Chevy turned the tables with an El Camino car-pickup to go up against the Ranchero.

At the small end of the scale, American Motors—focusing solely on compacts—built a record number of cars and earned a rewarding profit. Studebaker was in the throes of a comeback, courtesy of the compact Lark, viewed as a "new concept in motoring."

Analysts predicted a more stable market, courtesy of the now-required price stickers on new cars. Model-year auto output grew by 30.7 percent to more than 5.5 million. The federal gasoline tax was raised from three to four cents per gallon.

Chrysler dealers began to sell Simcas, imported from France. In addition to the expected Volkswagens, Renaults, and Austins, buyers could choose a Berkeley, NSU Prinz, Goggomobil, or Goliath, as well as a Citroen or Hillman—even a Skoda from Czechoslovakia or a Wartburg from East Germany. This year's convention of the National Automobile Dealers Association asked the vital question: "Are imported cars here to stay?"

Unemployment eased a bit, to 5.5 percent, after the great downfall of 1958. Overall inflation actually approached zero, though new cars cost 2.6 percent more as the model year began, and the average price paid for a new automobile rose sharply (to $3150). The average used car went for just over a thousand. Despite the economic downturn, average incomes of employed workers continued to rise, nearing $4600.

Rawhide and *Bonanza* entered TV screens for the first time, as did Rod Serling's *Twilight Zone*. Movies included *Anatomy of a Murder* with James Stewart, Billy Wilder's *Some Like It Hot*, Alfred Hitchcock's *North by Northwest*, and *On the Beach*.

Fidel Castro's troops moved into Havana, sending dictator Fulgencio Batista out of Cuba. Soviet leader Nikita Khrushchev toured the United States, stopping off at Disneyland—where he was denied entry for security reasons. Hawaii was admitted to the Union as the 50th state, and Charles Van Doren admitted having received answers beforehand on the popular quiz show *Twenty-One*.

Bobby Darin won a Grammy for his offbeat recording of "Mack the Knife," Johnny Mathis got "Misty," and Dion and the Belmonts warbled about "A Teenager in Love." Ace rock 'n' roller Buddy Holly was killed in a plane crash along with Ritchie Valens and The Big Bopper.

The Automobile Manufacturers Association announced that a crankcase-ventilation device would go on cars sold in California, effective on '61 models. Before long, emissions and safety issues would change both the way Americans thought about their cars as well as the way manufacturers built them.

Compacts would lead the way into the Sixties, followed by a fleet of mid-size models. Goliath full-size cars would not disappear for many years, and the horsepower race would gain in frenzy as "muscle cars" were added to the mix. Americans everywhere were about to face an even wider array of automotive choices.

American Motors Corporation

Top: Ed Anderson's design team struck gold with the beautifully proportioned, pillarless Custom Country Club, which was facelifted for '59.

Above: Ambassador sales improved to more than 23,000 units for 1959, as the nation eased out of its recession. All had the 327-cubic-inch V-8 carried over from '58. A Custom four-door sedan cost $2732.

Ambassador dashboards mimicked the design of lesser Ramblers, but were brushed with a bit more bright trim.

Replacing a traditional automatic-transmission shift lever was a Televac pushbutton control panel, which was mounted to the left side of the steering column. Similar to what Chrysler Corp. cars had used since 1956, Televac first appeared in '58, and continued as a Rambler feature into the Sixties.

A Rambler Custom six-cylinder sedan was a rather classy looking economy car—both inside and out.

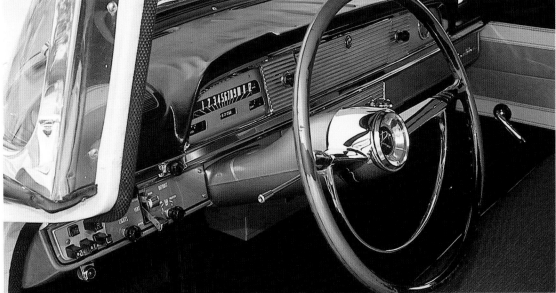

Added to the American line were two-door wagons, which, like the sedans, were merely resurrected from 1955. Only three of these enclosed sedan delivery versions were built. Interiors were decidedly stark next to those of upper-level Ramblers. American sales tripled in 1959, despite the fact that starting prices rose about $50 to $1821. Its success undoubtedly influenced the Big Three to come out with their own compact cars, which arrived en masse for 1960.

Metropolitan sales were also up dramatically for '59, prices holding at $1626 for the coupe, $1650 for the jaunty convertible. The Rambler nameplate would continue through the 1960s, to be replaced by the AMC badge in the '70s. But falling sales and mounting losses prompted a takeover by Renault of France in 1982. The last true AMCs were built in 1987, and the corporate name was soon relegated to history.

Above: Pretty in pink, a New Yorker convertible cost $4890 with its standard 413-cid 350-horsepower V-8. The grille retained a full-width look.

Above: An effective facelift adorned 1959 Chryslers, but the biggest change was underhood, as the mighty Hemi was no more. In its place was a conventional Golden Lion wedge-head V-8 of 383 or 413 cubic inches, which Chrysler justified as "a lighter, more efficient engine designed to give you better performance at the speeds you drive the most." Not mentioned is that it was also a heck-of-a-lot cheaper to build. New options for '59 included speed control, rear air suspension, and a swiveling driver's seat to ease entry.

Below: Following two seasons of simple brightwork applications, the '59 Windsor displayed a busier bodyside. The tall, imposing rear bumper was a departure from 1957-58. Entry-level Windsors carried a 383-cid V-8 good for 305 hp. This coupe went for $3289.

Bottom Right: Like other Chryslers, the 300-E lost its Hemi engine, but the 413-cid wedge-head that replaced it put out about the same horsepower: 380 standard, 390 optionally. The E carried over the D's front-end styling, but wore the new '59 tail treatment. By this time, sales were down to a trickle, at just 550 of the $5319 hardtops, and only 140 of the $5749 convertibles.

In a year when other Chrysler Corp. makes were up slightly, DeSoto sales continued to drop. Though somewhat higher for 1959, a total of 697 Adventurer orders could hardly be considered encouraging.

Speaking of Dodge, a new face graced the '59s, with heavily chromed eyebrows and a large loop bumper surrounding a mesh grille. Revised styling was "pointier" at each end, giving the car a more exaggerated look. This top-line Custom Royal Lancer coupe went for $3201.

V-8 choices included a 326 cubic incher with 255 horsepower, a 361 with 295-305 hp, and the new 383 shared with DeSoto that put out 320 hp in D-500 form, 345 in Super D-500 tune—which is the engine powering this loaded Custom Royal convertible that started at $3422.

The Adventurer was now a little less special; previously, it had always carried a more powerful engine than other DeSotos, but for '59, its 383-cubic-inch, 350-horsepower V-8 was also available on lesser models—and lower-priced Dodges.

For '59s like this Custom Royal Lancer convertible, headlamps were returned to the front sheetmetal, chrome wedges capped reshaped fins, and angle-cut bezels held rear lights.

Dodge wagons came in Custom and Sierra trim with six- or nine-passenger seating. Tailfin styling carried over from '58—and '57—and the bodies were shared by DeSoto and Plymouth. Prices ranged from $3103 to $3439.

The stately Crown Imperial limousine was the only '59 Chrysler Corp. car to remain powered by a Hemi; even the "civilian" Imperials switched to a wedge-head engine that year. A long-wheelbase sedan/limo had been offered by Chrysler since the early '30s, but sales had slowed to a trickle by this time, partly due to a staggering price: $15,075—more than three times that of a base Imperial. This is one of only seven '59s built. Surprisingly, the Crown Imperial continued into the mid 1960s, never selling more than 16 a year.

Above: A heavy, chromed grille and new headlight treatment distinguished the '59 Imperial. Power came from a 413-cubic-inch V-8 delivering 350 hp. The least expensive model in the line was this Custom Southampton coupe at $4910.

Below: At 129 inches, a $5774 Imperial Crown convertible rode a three-inch-longer wheelbase than its Chrysler New Yorker counterpart, giving it impressive stature.

Plymouth indeed got most of what was new at Chrysler Corp. for 1959. Back ends changed more than fronts, but the overall look was decidedly different than '58's. Hardtops and convertibles shared a compound-curve windshield that wrapped over at the top. Options included swivel bucket seats along with the fake spare tire cover introduced on Imperials the year before.

Above and Right: Sport Fury became the new top-line model for '59, offered only in hardtop coupe and convertible form priced at $2927 and $3125, respectively. Horsepower was curbed a bit for 1959, as the 318-cubic-inch V-8 standard in Sport Fury was tamed to 260, down 30 from its '58 peak.

Bottom: This 1959 Chrysler family portrait found the corporation in much the same position as it entered the decade, with offerings spanning the price spectrum from the low-price Plymouth to the high-end Imperial. Sadly, both of those makes have since departed: Imperial after 1975 (though the name would pop up now and again on luxury models of various descriptions), Plymouth in the early '00s, after being considered redundant—and inferior—to Dodge. Beating them both to the grave was DeSoto, which was celebrating its 30th anniversary as this photo was taken; it would not survive to celebrate its 33rd. Today, only Dodge and Chrysler remain—the two makes that originally merged under Walter P. Chrysler to form Chrysler Corp. in the late 1920s.

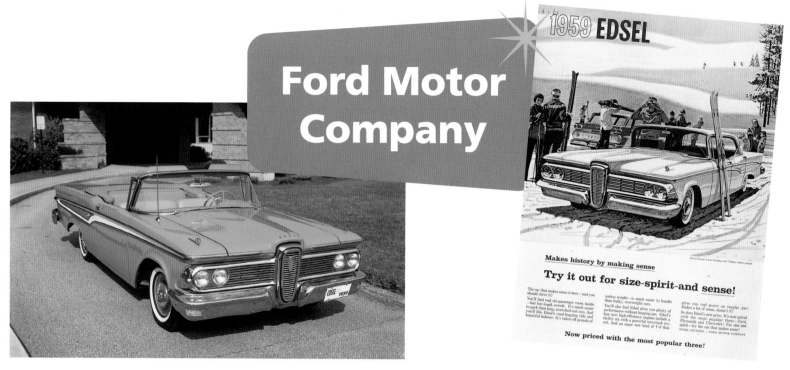

Ford Motor Company

In an effort to jump-start sales, Edsels received a number of changes for 1959. Among them was a new grille, which was a good thing, but it still incorporated the offensive "horse collar," which was not. The line was trimmed to just Ranger and Corsair, both now on the same wheelbase. The most expensive Edsel was this Corsair convertible, at $3072.

Ads claimed Edsels now made more sense, partially due to a newly standard six-cylinder engine, which had not been previously offered. V-8s of 292, 332, and 361 cid were available that provided from 200 to 303 horsepower, but 1958's big 410-cid V-8 was dropped—something that also perhaps "made more sense."

Upper Left: Edsel's tail treatment was altered as well, as shown on the make's cheapest model, the $2629 Ranger two-door sedan.

Lower Left: Station wagons became their own series for 1959, and as before, shared bodies with their Ford counterparts. Just one model was offered: the $2989 Villager, with six- or optional nine-passenger seating. All these 1959 changes didn't help, as sales fell by nearly 30 percent, sounding the Edsel's death knell. A handful of restyled 1960 models were sold before the poor Edsel was branded a failure and resigned to automotive history.

Below: Thunderbirds saw only minor trim changes for 1959, though newly optional was Lincoln's big 430-cubic-inch V-8 with 350 horsepower.

Above: Added for 1959 was the top-line Galaxie. Closed models, such as this $2582 four-door sedan, featured Thunderbird-like squared rear roof pillars. The top engine remained a 300-hp 352-cid V-8.

Below: Continental lost its separate-marque status for 1959, being folded into the Lincoln brand as the top-line model. Now called the Mark IV, it received only minor styling changes, including an altered side-cove treatment and rectangular taillights. The four-door hardtop listed for $6845, about $1250 to $1750 more than comparable Premiere and base-model siblings.

Station wagons continued as a separate series, topped by the woodgrained $2958 Country Squire. For the most part, Ford would spend the next four decades playing second fiddle to Chevrolet, as it continues to do today.

A reverse-slant opening backlight was just icing on the big, heavy cake.

Added to the Continental line was this $9208 formal sedan, with distinctive vinyl-covered top and thick rear roof pillars. Lincoln left the decade as it entered it, in second place behind Cadillac in the American luxury-car sweepstakes.

A Colony Park station wagon seated six. Note the woodgrain trim. Transmission tunnels shrunk in size for more legroom, accomplished by moving the engine and wheels forward.

Mercury's tailfin coves were extended forward for 1959, and the taillights they held were altered a bit. The grille was also restyled. Station wagons came in two- and four-door versions, with prices ranging from $3145 to $3932.

Above: Medalist was dropped for 1959, leaving Monterey, Montclair, and top-line Park Lane. This Montclair Cruiser four-door hardtop went for $3437.

Right: The available 430-cubic-inch V-8 was detuned to "only" 345 horsepower for 1959, and offered only in Park Lanes, like this $4031 Cruiser four-door hardtop. With the demise of Edsel in mid 1960, Mercury became Ford Motor Company's sole midprice line. It kept its distinct identity into the 1970s, during which the cars became little more than gussied-up Fords.

THE CAR: BUICK '59

LE SABRE
The thrilliest Buick

INVICTA
The most spirited Buick

ELECTRA
The most luxurious Buick

Here it is . . . and now you know! Know why we have called this THE CAR. Know that a new generation of great Buicks is truly now here. From just this one view you can see that here is not just new design . . . but splendidly right design for this day and age. A car that is lean and clean and stunningly low . . . and at the same time great in headroom and legroom, easy to get into or out of. And when you see your Buick dealer and walk the whole wonderful way around this Buick, you'll know still more how right all this is. From anywhere you look, here is a classic modern concept that is Buick speaking a new language of today. A language of fine cars priced within the reach of almost anyone. A language of quality and comfort and quiet pride of ownership . . . a language of performance satisfactions without equal. (see next page)

Above: In a stunning aesthetic reversal, Buick peeled chrome from its completely restyled '59s. Not so with tailfins, however, which increased in size and number. The rears became huge canted wings, a look that was mirrored in front. Model names were changed, too: LeSabre, Invicta, Electra, and Electra 225 made up the new order. The closed models depicted are four-door hardtops, which had a distinctive "flat-top" profile and huge wraparound rear window.

Below: An Electra 225 convertible that really did fly was the pace car for the 1959 running of the Indy 500. New for all Buicks but the entry-level LeSabre was a 325-horsepower 401-cubic-inch V-8; LeSabre kept the 250-hp 364. Buick's long-held "doctor's car" reputation sustained it through the end of the twentieth century and beyond, even if the cars bearing the Buick name weren't always the flamboyant carriages that closed out the '50s.

Above: Four-door pillared sedans had a completely different roofline that incorporated beautifully slender roof pillars and a conventional tapered look. This entry-level LeSabre sedan went for $2804.

Below: Nothing showed off Buick's new jet-age styling like a blazing red Electra 225 convertible. The $4192 ragtop seemed to be flying just standing still.

Towering tailfins with twin bullet taillights marked the 1959 Cadillacs—and made them famous. You could have a pair of your very own affixed to a Series 62 convertible for $5455.

Upper Left: Eldorado eschewed its traditional unique tailfins for more-pronounced versions of those found on lesser Caddys, thanks to a thick chrome trim strip that started at the windshield pillar and flowed to the tail. Eldorado's $7401 price added nearly $2000 to the cost of a comparable Series 62.

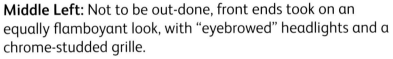

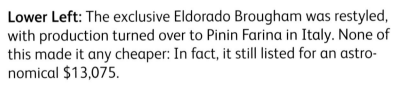

Middle Left: Not to be out-done, front ends took on an equally flamboyant look, with "eyebrowed" headlights and a chrome-studded grille.

Lower Left: The exclusive Eldorado Brougham was restyled, with production turned over to Pinin Farina in Italy. None of this made it any cheaper: In fact, it still listed for an astronomical $13,075.

Below: Cadillac's rocket-ship styling is modeled by a $7401 Eldorado Seville hardtop coupe. Cadillac remains GM's luxury division to this day, and typically leads all other domestic luxury cars in sales.

Chevy's "batwing" tailfins really stood out—in more ways than one. Impala was now a proper model perched at the top of the lineup, and this V-8 Impala convertible could have flown into your garage for $2967.

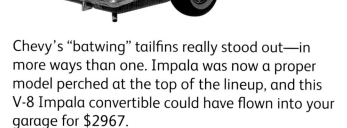

Since Chevrolets had been completely restyled for 1958 and then completely restyled again for '59, they were indeed "All New All Over Again," as this ad states. Depicted is the flat-top four-door hardtop, a roof style shared with other GM cars that year.

The midline Bel Air drew the most sales, and though a four-door hardtop was offered, the $2440 pillared sedan cost $116 less.

Above: Aside from stripping off the hood slats and trunk spears, there were few changes to the $3875 Corvette.

Upper Right: In a delayed reaction to the car-based Ford Ranchero that appeared two years earlier, 1959 saw the debut of the El Camino; a name—and concept—that would live on into the '80s. It was billed as "a vehicle combining ultra style with utility," and indeed it did. Chevrolet was the best-selling brand through most of the 1950s, and even in a changed market that has since seen an invasion of imports, it still holds that distinction today.

Lower Right: Like its GM siblings, Oldsmobiles were redesigned for 1959, gaining "Quiet power… extra safety… a Glide Ride… and Linear Look"—or so said the ads.

The "flat-top" four-door hardtop sedan looked particularly good dressed in Oldsmobile's aforesaid "Linear Look." This top-line Ninety-Eight version went for $4162 with the division's new 315-horsepower 394-cubic-inch V-8 that was shared with the Super 88.

Left: The Ninety-Eight convertible topped Oldsmobile's price scale at $4366.

Below: A Ninety-Eight pillared sedan listed for $3890, $272 less than its hardtop sibling. Oldsmobile would continue its reputation as an engineering leader through the 1960s, and for a couple of years in the '70s, produced the nation's best-selling car. But Olds began to lose its luster in the '80s as GM "genericized" its brands for cost savings, and after celebrating its 100th anniversary in 1997, was unceremoniously dropped after the 2004 model year. It was a sad end for what was once a brilliant star.

Left: A 1959 reskin brought the "Wide-Track Pontiac," a slogan the division would use well into the '60s. But it wasn't just advertising hype: Tread width increased by 4.5 inches in the rear and a whopping five inches in front. Adding visual width to a car that was already plenty wide enough was a low, split grille that tapered at the nose and extended fully across the front end. After a one-year hiatus for 1960, the split grille would return, becoming a Pontiac trademark that was used in one form or another on most of the division's cars through the 1980s, and graces every new Pontiac sold today. Shown is the top-line $3586 Bonneville convertible.

Right: The Bonneville series—which had previously consisted only of convertible and two-door hardtop "sporty" models—expanded to include a "flat-top" four-door hardtop sedan and even a station wagon for 1959. Low, wide taillight lenses mimicked the look in front, and were chosen for the same reason: to add the appearance of great girth. The flat-top sedan, two-door hardtop, and station wagon listed for $3333, $3257, and $3532, respectively.

Below: If a (rather costly) Bonneville wasn't in the cards, the $2704 price of entry to a Catalina four-door pillared sedan might be more palatable. A comparable midline Star Chief was about $300 more. All '59 Pontiacs were fitted with a larger 389-cubic-inch V-8 that put out 215 to 303 horsepower, or up to 345 hp with the triple two-barrel carburetor setup known as Tri-Power. Features such as a wide-track stance and powerful Tri-Power engines earned Pontiac a performance reputation that hit its stride during the Sixties, and continues to this day.

Studebaker-Packard Corporation

Right: Studebaker dropped its "regular sized" cars for 1959 and put all its money on the compact Lark. Larks were considerably shorter and lighter than their predecessors, but still offered ample interior room—as this ad strives to show. Base engine in the Lark VI was the little 169-cubic-inch six resurrected from '54, now rated at 90 horsepower. The 259-cid V-8, providing 180 to 195 hp, was standard in the Lark VIII.

Below: Released during an economic recession, the compact Lark replaced Studebaker's standard line—and more than doubled the company's sales. Six-cylinder models, called Lark VI, brought back the smaller 169 6-cid L-head six last used in '54, now making 90 horsepower. Though Larks started as low as $1925—about $250 less than the cheapest Chevy—this flashy Lark VI hardtop was a little more precious at $2275.

Most expensive of the Larks was the Lark VIII two-door wagon at $2590. Lark wagons came only in two-door versions for '59. Offered in DeLuxe or Regal trim with six-cylinder or V-8 power, they rode a longer wheelbase than other Larks, 113 inches versus 108.5.

The Loewy coupes carried on sans the hardtop Golden Hawk version for 1959. Pillared Silver Hawks were available in six-cylinder form for $2360 and with the 259-cubic-inch V-8 for $2495. Though sales would never again top 9000 units a year, the Hawk would live on almost as long as Studebaker itself. Larks, by contrast, would prove enormously popular (at least by Studebaker standards), and would keep the company aloft until the volley of compacts from other American manufacturers finally shot it down in 1966, killing Studebaker along with it.